MW01537460

Alex Morgan
Biography For Kids

Motivational Story of American Female
Soccer Player to Inspire Big Dreamers

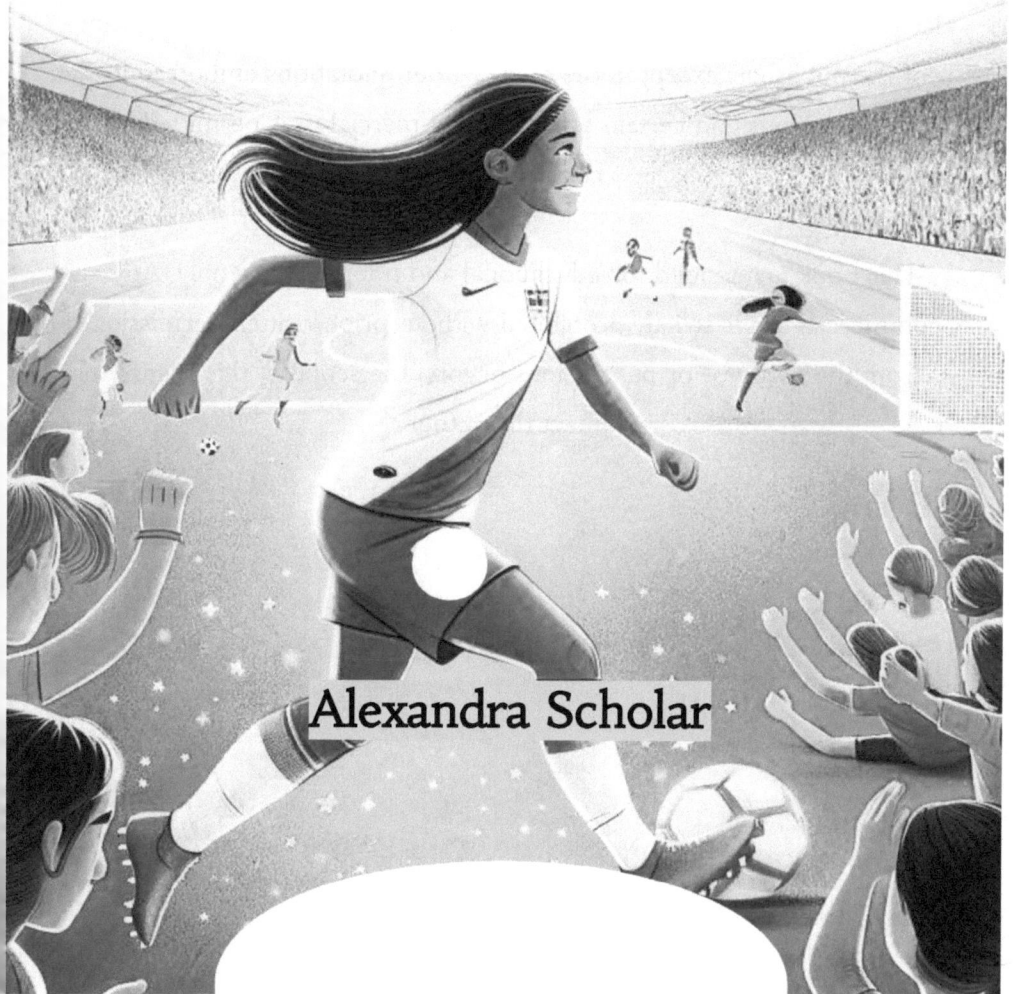

Alexandra Scholar

Copyright © 2024 Alexandra Scholar.

No part of this book may be reproduced, distributed, or transmitted in any form or by any means, including photocopying, recording, or other electronic or mechanical methods, without the prior written permission of the publisher, except in the case of brief quotations embodied in critical reviews and certain other noncommercial uses permitted by copyright law.

This book is intended for educational and nonprofit use only. Any commercial use is strictly prohibited without prior written permission from the author. For permissions beyond the scope of this license, contact the author.

Table of Contents

TABLE OF CONTENTS   2

INTRODUCTION   4

CHAPTER 1: A STAR IS BORN   8

CHAPTER 2: THE SOCCER FIELD BECOMES HOME   22

CHAPTER 3: RISING THROUGH THE RANKS   40

CHAPTER 4: WORLD CUP DREAMS   56

CHAPTER 5: OLYMPIC GLORY   70

CHAPTER 6: BECOMING A ROLE MODEL   80

CHAPTER 7: BALANCING FAMILY AND CAREER   90

CHAPTER 8: LEADING THE TEAM   104

CHAPTER 9: WORLD CUP CHAMPIONS AGAIN!   118

CHAPTER 10: OVERCOMING ADVERSITY   126

CHAPTER 11: FIGHTING FOR EQUAL PAY   138

CHAPTER 12: ALEX MORGAN OFF THE FIELD   152

CHAPTER 13: WHAT MAKES ALEX MORGAN SPECIAL   164

CHAPTER 14: ALEX MORGAN'S LEGACY   176

INTRODUCTION

> *"Dream big, because dreams do come true!" - Alex Morgan*

Is scoring a goal at the World Cup something you've ever fantasized about? Or how about leading your squad to a triumph and wearing the glittering gold medal around your neck. Get ready for an incredible tale involving a real-life superhero named Alex Morgan!

Alex isn't your typical soccer player; she's a total rock star with cleats! She can sprint like a cheetah with a rocket strapped on, unleash kicks with the power of a mama bear protecting her cubs, and her smile is infectious enough to light up a whole stadium. But way back before all the trophies and roaring crowds, Alex was just a regular kid with a dream bigger than a beach ball.

Growing up in sunny California, Alex craved adventure. She'd race around like a blur, playing every sport she could find. But soccer was the one that truly sparked a fire in her soul.

4

She'd weave across the field like a magician dribbling the ball, leaving defenders in her dust and rocketing goals into the net!

As Alex grew older, her talent blossomed like a wildflower. She played on all sorts of teams, from her neighborhood crew to fancy club championships. And guess what? She even rocketed her way onto the U.S. Women's National Team, the most incredible soccer squad on the entire planet! Talk about a dream come true!

Being a superstar athlete isn't always sunshine and lollipops, though. Alex faced her share of rainy days. There were injuries that sidelined her for what felt like forever, games where her team just couldn't seem to catch a break, and even some folks who doubted her. But you know what? Alex never let those things dim her light. She practiced like a champion, held her head high, and never stopped chasing her dreams with the heart of a lion.

And guess what? It totally paid off! Alex helped her team hoist the World Cup trophy not just once, but a whopping TWO TIMES! She even drilled a goal that helped them snag the gold medal at the Olympics! That's like winning the Super

Bowl and the NBA Finals all in the same year – pretty mind-blowing, right?

But Alex is so much more than just a phenomenal athlete. She's also a total inspiration to kids of all ages. She uses her voice to fight for what's right, like making sure girls who play sports get treated just as amazingly as boys. She also has a big heart for helping others and making a positive impact in her community.

Are you prepared to be swept away by the extraordinary tale of Alex Morgan? Inspiring, hilarious, and sure to make you laugh till your sides hurt, this awesome soccer star illustrates that anything is possible with determination, perseverance, and a whole lot of heart! Now is the moment to fasten your shoes and embark with Alex on an unforgettable journey!

Chapter 1: A Star is Born

> *"Follow your dreams and believe in yourself. Anything is possible."*
> *- Alex Morgan*

Growing Up in Diamond Bar

At Diamond Bar, the sun appeared to always be a little bit brighter and the laughter a little bit louder. Alex Morgan, a future soccer sensation, spent her youth in this sunny paradise. Her days were filled with the kind of adventures that make you want to jump out of bed in the morning and shout, "Let's go!"

From the moment Alex could toddle, she was a little whirlwind of energy. She'd zoom around the house, leaving a trail of toys and giggles in her wake. Her parents often joked that she had a built-in motor, always revving to go, go, go! She'd climb trees like a monkey, build forts with blankets and pillows, and chase butterflies with a net held high.

The Morgan house was rarely quiet. Alex and her two older sisters, Jeni and Jeri, were a trio of troublemakers, always up for a challenge or a prank. They'd turn the living room into a gymnastics studio, using the couch as a trampoline and the coffee table as a balance beam. They'd organize backyard Olympics, competing in events like the "fastest lemonade chug" and the "longest watermelon seed spit."

But it wasn't all fun and games. Alex was a curious kid, always asking questions and eager to learn. She loved reading books about faraway lands, imagining herself as an explorer discovering hidden treasures. She'd spend hours poring over maps, tracing her fingers along the lines and dreaming of traveling the world.

Alex also had a creative streak. She'd draw pictures of fantastical creatures, write stories about talking animals, and even put on plays for her family and friends. She loved expressing herself through art and storytelling, letting her imagination run wild.

But no matter what she was doing, Alex always had a smile on her face. She was a natural leader, always rallying her friends and siblings for new adventures. She had a way of making everyone feel included and valued, turning ordinary days into extraordinary memories.

Even as a young girl, Alex had a competitive spirit. She loved playing games, whether it was board games with her family or sports with her friends. She always strived to be the best, but not in a way that made others feel bad. She simply wanted to challenge herself and see how far she could push her limits.

Diamond Bar was more than simply a place to hang out and have fun; it was a place where she shaped her character and found her hobbies. Being a part of a team, sticking with it, and keeping a positive outlook are all things Alex picked up.

A Love for Sports

As a child, Alex didn't only have an interest in sports; they were her world. Her boundless energy and passion made her seem like a miniature whirlwind. If only you could capture and market her undying love for sports, you'd be as wealthy as a Halloween candy store owner.

Every day was an opportunity for Alex to play. Every morning, she would greet the day with enthusiasm, poised to face whatever obstacle lay ahead. She would be more energized to tackle the field, court, or track than a superhero getting into their costume, and she would fasten her sneakers.

There was no sport Alex wouldn't try. She'd dribble a basketball like a Harlem Globetrotter, swing a softball bat like a baseball pro, and even try her hand at gymnastics, cartwheeling across the lawn like a tumbling tumbleweed. She was a natural athlete, with quick reflexes and a knack for picking up new skills.

Being good in sports wasn't the only reason Alex loved them. It celebrated the pleasure of movement, the excitement of competition, and the satisfaction of learning and performing a new skill. Hearing the ball whizz through the net, the crash of the bat hitting the ball, and the crowd's screams as she crossed the finish line were all sounds that brought her great joy.

When she wasn't playing sports, Alex was watching them. She'd glue herself to the TV, soaking up every detail of her favorite athletes' performances. She'd analyze their techniques, study their strategies, and dream of one day playing alongside them.

Alex, though, was more than simply a sports fan; she was an athlete. She would construct impromptu miniature golf courses, basketball hoops, and soccer fields in her backyard. In her spontaneous games, which she would host for her brothers and friends, she would turn mundane afternoons into grand shows of strategy and talent.

Alex's love for sports was contagious. She inspired her friends and siblings to join her in her athletic pursuits, creating a community of active, healthy kids who loved to play and have fun. They'd challenge each other, cheer each other on, and celebrate each other's victories, creating bonds that would last a lifetime.

Alex tried a lot of other sports, but soccer was the one that she ended up falling in love with. The thrill of scoring goals, working as a team, and the constant motion were all things that drew her in. With remarkable agility, a strong shot, and lightning-fast speed, she was a natural on the field.

Early Signs of Talent

Think of young Alex, who isn't quite ten years old, navigating a group of larger children like a squirrel on a caffeine high, with the soccer ball stuck to her foot. It wasn't a matter of chance or sorcery; it was an epiphany of raw ability, a lightning bolt that had parents and coaches alike saying, "Wow, that kid's got something special!"

From the very first time she stepped onto a soccer field, Alex was a force of nature. She wasn't the biggest or the strongest, but she had something else – a fire in her belly and a twinkle in her eye that screamed, "I'm here to play!" She'd sprint down the field like a cheetah chasing its dinner, leaving defenders in her dust.

But it wasn't just about speed. Alex had a sixth sense for the game. She'd know where to be before the ball even got there, like she had a secret radar guiding her every move. She could read the field like a book, anticipating her teammates' passes and predicting her opponents' next move. It was like she was playing chess while everyone else was playing checkers.

The inherent talent that Alex possessed astounded her coaches. Alex stood out from the other gifted children they had observed. She wasn't only competent; she was ravenous. She aspired to improve herself by acquiring knowledge and expanding her horizons. Their words of wisdom would be like water to her, and she would be quick to put them into action.

But Alex's talent wasn't just about her physical skills and her soccer smarts. It was also about her attitude. She was a team player, always cheering on her teammates and encouraging them to do their best. She didn't get discouraged by mistakes; instead, she used them as learning opportunities, figuring out how to do better next time.

And let's not forget her competitive spirit. Alex loved to win, but she loved to play even more. She'd dive for loose balls, chase down opponents, and never give up until the final whistle blew. She was like a little Energizer Bunny, always going and going and going.

Even at a young age, Alex was a leader. She'd rally her teammates when they were down, inspire them with her infectious energy, and always find a way to make the game fun. She wasn't just a talented soccer player; she was a spark plug, igniting a passion for the game in everyone around her.

Alex's early success wasn't just about winning trophies and accolades; it was about discovering her love for the game and realizing her potential. She learned that hard work, dedication, and a positive attitude can take you far in life, both on and off the field.

The little girl who once ran around the backyard, kicking a soccer ball with her friends, was blossoming into a true star. Her talent was undeniable, her passion was contagious, and her future was as bright as the California sun. The world was her oyster, and she was ready to shuck it open and show everyone what she was made of.

Alex loved to play all sorts of sports as a kid. What are your favorite activities or things you love to do?

_____

_____

_____

_____

_____

_____

Even though she tried different sports, soccer became Alex's passion. Have you ever discovered something you really love doing? What makes it special for you?

_____

_____

_____

_____

_____

_____

Alex's family was very supportive of her playing sports. Who are the people in your life who encourage and cheer you on?

_____
_____
_____
_____
_____
_____

What do you think it means to have a "spark" or a special talent? Do you think you have a spark for something?

_____
_____
_____
_____
_____
_____

Alex always had fun while playing sports. What do you think is the most important thing to remember when trying new things or playing games?

_____
_____
_____
_____

_____
_____

Who are the people in your life who make up your "team"?
Write down their names and what they do to support you.

_____
_____
_____
_____

_____
_____

IMAGINE YOU'RE STANDING ON A PODIUM, RECEIVING A GOLD MEDAL FOR SOMETHING YOU'RE PASSIONATE ABOUT. WHAT IS IT? DRAW A PICTURE OF YOURSELF ACHIEVING THIS DREAM.

Chapter 2: The Soccer Field Becomes Home

> *The only way to prove that you're a good sport is to lose." -*
> *Ernie Banks*

Joining Club Teams

Alex Morgan started to make a name for herself in the Diamond Bar soccer divisions as she matured and honed her abilities. People couldn't stop raving about her incredible speed, agility, and goal-scoring skills. Nonetheless, Alex was aware that she needed to push herself farther if she aspired to elevate her performance. When she realized she could play on club teams with some of the area's top youth players, she made the decision to do so.

Joining a club team was a big step for Alex. It meant more intense practices, tougher competition, and a lot of travel. But Alex was ready for the challenge. She was determined to improve her skills and show that she could compete at the highest levels. Her parents were incredibly supportive, willing to make the sacrifices necessary to help her pursue her dreams.

Cypress Elite was one of Alex's first club teams; they were famous for having great players and were often in the thick of things. An electric current of anticipation coursed through Alex the second she set foot on the field. She adored the game despite its significantly higher degree of difficulty compared to her previous experiences. She had to work really hard during practices to become in better shape, sharpen her skills, and understand the game better.

Alex became well-known very fast at Cypress Elite. Her work ethic and capacity to learn and adapt were lauded by her instructors. She practiced dribbling, shooting, and passing relentlessly, arriving early and staying late every day. Her teammates saw her hard work and commitment and immediately embraced her as an integral part of the squad.

Playing for a club team also meant participating in numerous tournaments, both locally and nationally. These tournaments were thrilling opportunities for Alex to showcase her skills. The competition was fierce, with teams from all over the country coming to compete. Alex thrived in this environment, using every game as a chance to learn and grow.

For Alex and her squad, competing in the esteemed Surf Cup was an unforgettable experience. Attracting top teams from throughout the country, the Surf Cup is a prestigious youth soccer competition held in San Diego. Alex felt a mix of enthusiasm and anxiety, but she was prepared to give it her all. Extremely high stakes and elite level competition made for tough games.

On one occasion, with time running down in a match, Alex's squad found themselves down a goal. Alex maintained her composure under severe strain. Her lightning-fast dribbling allowed her to get the ball past two defenders, and she scored the game-tying goal after receiving a feed from a teammate. A wave of delight and pride washed over Alex as her comrades burst into shouts. Such experiences strengthened her conviction that one could triumph over any challenge with perseverance and focus.

While playing for club teams, Alex also learned the importance of teamwork and leadership. She discovered that being a great player wasn't just about individual skills, but also about working together with her teammates to achieve common goals. She developed strong bonds with her teammates, both on and off the field, and became known for her positive attitude and encouraging spirit.

As Alex continued to play for club teams, her talent and hard work caught the attention of college scouts. They saw in her a player with immense potential, someone who could make a significant impact at the collegiate level. This was an exciting time for Alex, as she began to receive offers from top college soccer programs. She knew that her dream of playing soccer at the highest level was within reach, but she also understood that she had to stay focused and keep working hard.

Berkeley was one of several universities that took an interest in Alex. In addition to its stellar academic reputation, the school boasted a formidable soccer program. The opportunity to play for the Berkeley soccer team delighted Alex, and he committed to the squad. This choice was a watershed moment in her path; it signaled that she was ready to level up.

Joining club teams was a pivotal moment in Alex Morgan's soccer journey. It challenged her to push her limits, taught her valuable lessons about teamwork and leadership, and opened doors to new opportunities. Through it all, Alex remained dedicated to her dreams, constantly striving to be the best player she could be.

Developing Skills and Strategy

Club soccer was more than just a game to Alex; it was an opportunity to discover her latent abilities and develop into a soccer ninja. Think about this: Walking out onto the field for her inaugural club practice, Alex's eyes gleam with resolve. It felt as if you were entering a clandestine soccer academy, where masters of the game developed their talents to a finer degree.

The coaches acted as knowledgeable guides, leading Alex and her teammates in skill-enhancing drills and exercises. They'd show them the ropes of dribbling, passing the ball deftly between defenders and cones. They would instruct them in the art of the exact pass, which would launch the ball into the air and find an eager colleague waiting below. They would also instruct them in the finer points of shooting, allowing them to unleash powerful blows that could propel the ball into the net with incredible velocity.

Alex was like a sponge, soaking up every bit of knowledge her coaches shared. She'd practice for hours, her legs burning, her lungs gasping for air, but she wouldn't stop until she got it right. She'd juggle the ball, dribble through obstacle courses, and practice shooting until her toes were numb.

Physical abilities weren't the only determinant, though. Alex had to hone her soccer acumen as well. Similar to putting together a jigsaw on the field, she gained knowledge of various formations. She knew how to out-plan and outmanoeuvre her opponents by studying their strengths and flaws. She mastered the art of game reading, which allowed her to anticipate her teammates' actions and the ball's trajectory.

It was like playing a giant game of chess, but instead of pawns and bishops, there were strikers and defenders. Alex had to think strategically, making split-second decisions that could mean the difference between victory and defeat.

Not only did Alex pick up tips from her coaches, but she also picked up pointers from her teammates. In doing so, they would encourage one another to improve. As well as supporting one another through difficult times, they would rejoice in one another's triumphs. Their shared passion for the game brought them closer together as a family and a team.

Every practice was a new adventure for Alex. She'd learn new skills, try new strategies, and discover new ways to express herself on the field. She'd experiment with different positions, playing striker, midfielder, and even defender, figuring out where she fit best and how she could contribute to the team.

Not every step was smooth sailing. When the ball refused to comply or when Alex's passes failed to connect, there were days when she felt irritated. From time to time, she questioned if she has the skills necessary to compete at this level. However, she persevered. She never stopped trying to improve herself via training and education.

Balancing School and Sports

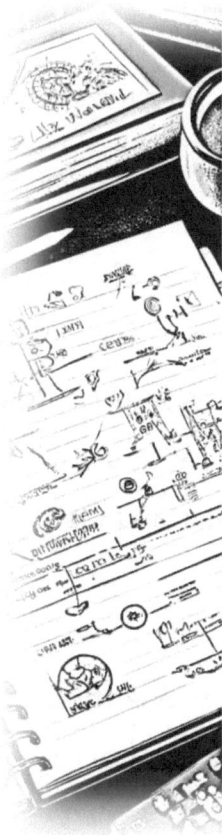

Balancing school and sports was one of the biggest challenges Alex Morgan faced as she grew up. Imagine having to juggle hours of soccer practice, intense games, homework, and studying for tests. It might sound overwhelming, but Alex managed to do it all with a smile and a determination that was truly inspiring.

From a young age, Alex knew that education was just as important as soccer. Her parents always emphasized the value of doing well in school, and Alex took this to heart. She was determined to excel both on the field and in the classroom. This meant she had to be very organized and disciplined with her time.

Alex's typical day started early in the morning. She would wake up, eat a healthy breakfast, and get ready for school. During the school day, she paid close attention in class, took notes, and participated actively. She understood that staying focused during school hours would help her manage her homework and studies more efficiently later.

After school, Alex would head straight to soccer practice. These practices were intense, often lasting several hours.

They included drills to improve her skills, fitness training to keep her in top shape, and scrimmages to work on team strategies. Despite the physical and mental demands, Alex loved every minute of it. Soccer was her passion, and she was willing to put in the hard work required to get better.

When practice ended, Alex's day was far from over. She would return home, eat dinner with her family, and then dive into her homework. Balancing school and sports meant that Alex had to make the most of every minute. She developed a routine that helped her stay on top of her assignments and studies.

Alex prioritized her work as one of her techniques. She would make a prioritized list of all her homework and study objectives, and then get to the most pressing ones. Using this method, she was able to keep up with her studies even when her soccer schedule got crazy. Time management was another skill she picked up; she now has certain periods of the day for things like studying, relaxing, and soccer practice.

There were times when balancing school and sports was incredibly tough. Alex had to miss out on social events with friends, late-night hangouts, and sometimes even family gatherings to keep up with her responsibilities. However, she never complained. She knew that sacrifices were necessary to achieve her dreams. Her friends and family understood her dedication and supported her every step of the way.

Despite her busy schedule, Alex always found joy in both her schoolwork and soccer. She loved learning new things in class, whether it was a complex math problem or a fascinating history lesson. Her curiosity and love for knowledge kept her motivated. Similarly, every soccer practice and game was an opportunity to improve, compete, and enjoy the sport she loved so much.

Alex's teachers and coaches played a significant role in helping her balance her commitments. They admired her dedication and often provided extra support when needed. Her teachers were understanding when she had to travel for games, allowing her to make up for missed work. Her coaches, on the other hand, encouraged her to excel academically, knowing that a well-rounded education was crucial for her future.

Throughout high school, Alex's commitment to balancing school and sports never wavered. Her hard work paid off in both areas. On the soccer field, she became a standout player, earning numerous accolades and catching the attention of college scouts. In the classroom, she maintained excellent grades, proving that it was possible to excel in both academics and athletics.

Receiving a scholarship offer from Berkeley was one of the most fulfilling moments for Alex. The academic prowess and robust soccer program at this esteemed institution were well-known. All of Alex's hard work juggling academics and athletics paid off when he accepted the offer. While attending university, she was overjoyed to continue playing soccer at the collegiate level.

College brought a new set of challenges for Alex. The level of competition in soccer was higher, and the academic demands were even greater. But by then, Alex had honed her time management skills and was ready to take on the challenge. She continued to prioritize her tasks, stay organized, and work hard both on and off the field.

At Berkeley, Alex's typical day was even more demanding. Mornings were filled with classes, where she absorbed new knowledge and tackled assignments. Afternoons were dedicated to rigorous soccer practices, pushing her physical and mental limits. Evenings were spent studying and completing homework. Despite the grueling schedule, Alex never lost sight of her goals.

Her experiences at Berkeley further shaped her as a student-athlete. She learned to collaborate with her teammates and classmates, developing strong bonds and friendships. The support system she built around her helped her navigate the challenges of balancing school and sports. Her professors and coaches continued to provide guidance and encouragement, recognizing her dedication and potential.

Throughout her college years, Alex continued to excel. Her hard work on the soccer field earned her a spot on the U.S. Women's National Team, an incredible achievement that brought her one step closer to her dreams. Her academic success laid a strong foundation for her future, proving that she could excel in any endeavor she chose to pursue.

Alex joined club teams to improve her soccer skills. Have you ever joined a club, team, or group to learn something new or get better at something you enjoy?

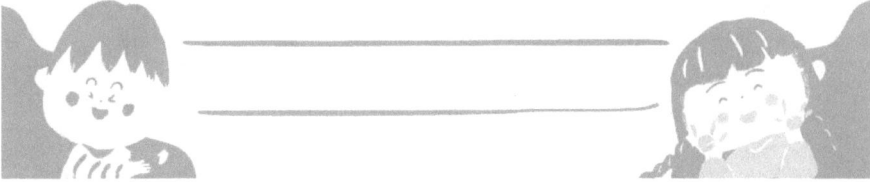

_____

_____

_____

_____

_____

_____

Balancing school and sports was a challenge for Alex. What are some of the challenges you face when trying to balance the things you have to do with the things you want to do?

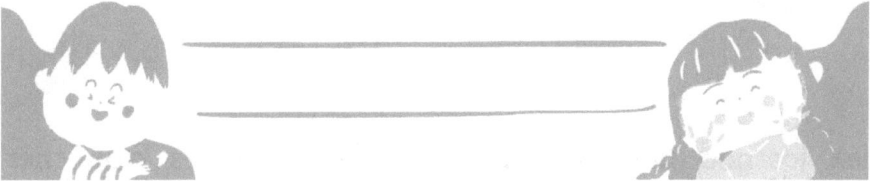

_____

_____

_____

_____

_____

Alex loved the feeling of being part of a team. When have you felt like you were part of a team? What made it feel that way?

_____

_____

_____

_____

_____

_____

What does it mean to be a "team player"? How can you be a good teammate in your own activities or games?

_____

_____

_____

_____

_____

_____

Alex learned new soccer skills and strategies from her coaches. Who are some people in your life who teach you new things?

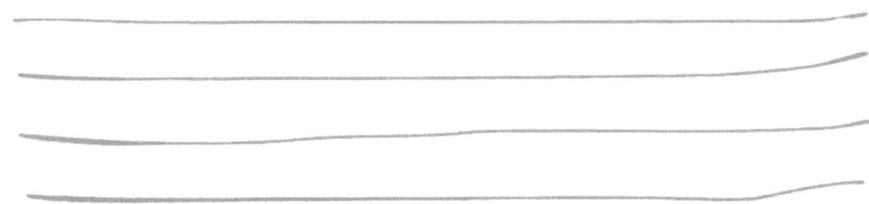

Chapter 3: Rising Through the Ranks

> *"Champions keep playing until they get it right." - Billie Jean King*

High School Standout

Like a rollercoaster, high school is full of curveballs and shocks. At the same moment, Alex's soccer career took off, soaring into orbit like a rocket. Her status has elevated her from that of an average player to that of a superstar and formidable opponent.

Think of a stadium full of people, all pumped up and ready to go. Everything is buzzing with energy; you can almost taste it, the lights are dazzling, and the atmosphere is electrifying. In spite of her racing heart, Alex takes a long breath. The grass feels chilly under her cleats as she strides onto the field. The game begins as soon as the whistle sounds!

Alex was a natural leader on the field. She'd weave through defenders like a magician, her footwork so quick and precise it was like watching a dance. She'd pass the ball with pinpoint accuracy, setting up her teammates for goals. And when she got a chance to shoot, watch out! Her shots were like lightning bolts, sizzling past the goalie and into the back of the net.

But Alex wasn't just a goal scorer; she was a playmaker, a strategist, a conductor of the soccer orchestra. She could read the game like a book, anticipating her opponents' moves and directing her teammates with a flick of her wrist or a nod of her head. She was the engine that powered her team, the spark that ignited their passion.

The news of Alex's abilities quickly spread. Many college coaches came to see her play in an effort to get her services. Alex stood out to them because of his exceptional leadership qualities, athleticism, and skill set. They were aware of her inevitable brilliance.

But Alex wasn't just a star on the soccer field; she was also a star in the classroom. She was a straight-A student, a member of the honor roll, and a role model for her peers. She knew that education was important, just as important as soccer. It was the foundation upon which she could build her future.

Balancing school and sports wasn't easy, but Alex made it look like a breeze. She was like a juggling act, keeping all the balls in the air at once. She'd study in the car on the way to games, squeeze in homework assignments during lunch breaks, and stay up late to finish projects.

Still, the effort was worthwhile. On and off the pitch, Alex was successful because of his hard effort. Her athletic and intellectual accomplishments garnered her a plethora of honors and medals. She was honored with the title of Gatorade National Player of the Year, which is given to the nation's top high school athlete.

There was more to Alex's accomplishment than personal bragging rights. The focus was on the group, the institution, and the neighborhood. Her teammates gave it their all, her students pushed themselves to their limits, and her town came out to support their beloved athletes.

The four years that Alex spent in high school were filled with adventure, hardship, and success. She found her potential, established friends for life, and gained wisdom. Everyone who knew her saw her as exceptional, a pioneer, an example to follow, and a source of motivation.

As Alex prepared to graduate from high school, she knew that her journey was just beginning. The world was her oyster, and she was ready to shuck it open and show everyone what she was made of. The next chapter of her life was about to begin, and it promised to be even more exciting than the last.

College Recruitment

College coaches weren't just watching Alex's games; they were practically drooling over her talent. It was like a candy shop owner seeing a kid with a giant bag of money—they wanted her on their team! Letters, emails, and phone calls flooded in, each one promising a scholarship, a chance to play at the next level, a path to the big leagues.

Alex was like a kid in a candy store, but instead of lollipops and chocolate bars, she was surrounded by opportunities. Each college had its own unique flavor: some were big and flashy, like a jawbreaker, while others were small and cozy, like a chocolate truffle. Some had a long history of soccer success, like a classic candy cane, while others were up-and-coming, like a new sour gummy flavor.

Choosing a college was like picking out the perfect outfit for a party. You had to consider the style, the fit, and how it made you feel. Alex visited different campuses, met with coaches and players, and tried to envision herself as part of each team.

Some colleges were like a party with all the bells and whistles, promising fame, fortune, and a chance to play in front of thousands of fans. Others were more like a family gathering, offering a close-knit community, individual attention, and a chance to grow as a player and a person.

Alex listened to her heart, her gut, and her head. She weighed the pros and cons, talked to her parents and coaches, and even made a list of her top choices. It was like a scavenger hunt, searching for the perfect place to call home for the next four years.

In the end, Alex chose the University of California, Berkeley. It wasn't the biggest or the flashiest school, but it felt right. The coaches believed in her, the players welcomed her with open arms, and the campus had a warm, inviting vibe.

Alex's college years were like a roller coaster ride, full of ups and downs, twists and turns. She faced new challenges, both on and off the field. The competition was tougher, the expectations were higher, and the pressure was intense.

Alex, nevertheless, was not the kind to back down from a fight. She accepted it and used it to motivate herself to improve. She trained smarter, learned more, and practiced harder. She mastered the art of time management, juggling several responsibilities, and setting priorities.

Alex's college career was like a highlight reel, filled with amazing goals, breathtaking assists, and unforgettable victories. She became a star player for the California Golden Bears, leading them to multiple conference championships and NCAA tournament appearances.

The key to Alex's success, though, was not her own efforts alone. Everything revolved on the squad, the friendships, and the mutual love of the game. She was like a sister to her teammates, always there to cheer them on and console them when they were down.

College was more than just a stepping stone for Alex; it was a transformative experience. She grew as a player, a student, and a person. She learned valuable lessons about teamwork, leadership, and perseverance. She discovered her true potential and realized that her dreams were within reach.

Making the National Team

Instead of the sugar trees and rivers of chocolate you'd find at Willy Wonka's chocolate factory, picture yourself receiving a golden ticket to play soccer for the greatest team in the world. And that is exactly what happened when the US Women's National Team extended an invitation to Alex Morgan to try out. This is a once in a lifetime chance!

It wasn't as simple as walking out onto the field and declaring, "I'm here!" so calm down, everyone. Yeah, Alex had to show her worth. She had to prove to the coaches that she could compete at the highest level and represent her nation with honor.

The tryouts were like a super-intense boot camp for soccer ninjas. The best of the best were there, all vying for a spot on the team. Alex had to push herself harder than she ever had before, juggling school, soccer practice, and the pressure of performing under the watchful eyes of the coaches.

Every drill was like a test, every scrimmage a battle. Alex had to show off her speed, her agility, her ball control, and her tactical awareness. She had to prove that she could work with others, communicate effectively, and adapt to different situations.

Alex was like a sponge, soaking up every bit of feedback from the coaches. She'd analyze her performance, identify areas for improvement, and work tirelessly to get better. She'd stay late after practice, putting in extra hours on the field and in the gym.

However, practicing wasn't the only thing. Like Alex, she had to show her worth in games. She faced up against some of the world's top players in exhibition matches against other national teams. It felt like something out of a video game, as Alex faced off against formidable foes from all around the world.

But Alex wasn't intimidated. She embraced the challenge, using it as an opportunity to show what she was made of. She played with her heart on her sleeve, never backing down, always fighting for every ball. She scored goals, made assists, and helped her team win games.

After months of grueling tryouts and intense competition, the moment of truth arrived. The coaches gathered the players together to announce their decision. Alex held her breath, her heart pounding in her chest. The coach called out the names of the players who had made the team, and there it was – Alex Morgan!

The feeling of joy and accomplishment was overwhelming. Alex had done it! She had achieved her dream of playing for the U.S. Women's National Team. It was like winning the lottery, but instead of money, she had earned the chance to represent her country on the world stage.

But Alex knew that this was just the beginning. The hard work was far from over. She had to continue to push herself, to improve her skills, and to earn her place on the team. But she was ready for the challenge. She had a fire in her belly, a twinkle in her eye, and a dream in her heart.

Alex worked hard in high school to get noticed by college recruiters. What are some goals you're working towards now? How are you working hard to achieve them?

_____

_____

_____

_____

_____

_____

Alex had to make a big decision about which college to attend. Have you ever had to make a tough choice? How did you decide what was best for you?

_____

_____

_____

_____

_____

_____

Playing for the national team was a dream come true for Alex. What is a dream you have for yourself? What steps can you take to make it happen?

_____

_____

_____

_____

_____

_____

What do you think it takes to become a "standout" in something you love doing? Is it just talent, or are there other important qualities?

_____

_____

_____

_____

_____

Alex had to balance her schoolwork with her soccer commitments. How do you balance the things you need to

do with the things you want to do? What are some strategies
you use?

_____

_____

_____

_____

_____

_____

DRAW A LADDER AND WRITE DOWN YOUR BIG DREAM AT THE TOP. THEN, FILL IN THE STEPS YOU NEED TO TAKE TO REACH THAT DREAM.

Chapter 4: World Cup Dreams

> *"It's not whether you get knocked down; it's whether you get up." - Vince Lombardi*

Training for the Biggest Stage

Just picture yourself receiving an official invitation to join Hogwarts, the world's preeminent academy for wizards and witches. When Alex learned she had been selected to play for the United States Women's National Team, it was much like that! Receiving that golden ticket was like winning the lottery for the most fantastic soccer journey imaginable. Like Hogwarts, though, there was some significant training that had to take place.

Training for the World Cup was like preparing for an epic quest. Alex and her teammates had to level up their skills, become stronger, faster, and smarter. They had to learn new spells, I mean, strategies, and become masters of the soccer pitch.

The training wasn't just about kicking the ball around; it was like a superhero boot camp. They'd run until their legs felt like jelly, lift weights until their muscles screamed for mercy, and practice drills until they could do them blindfolded (though they didn't actually wear blindfolds, that would be silly).

Every day was a new challenge, a chance to push their limits and become the best they could be. They'd wake up before the sun even thought about yawning, eat a breakfast fit for champions, and hit the field with a fire in their bellies.

The coaches were like master trainers, pushing the players to their limits but always with a twinkle in their eye. They'd come up with crazy drills, like dribbling through a maze of cones while wearing goofy goggles, or juggling the ball while balancing on a wobbly platform. It was all about testing their skills and building their confidence.

Alex thrived in this environment. She was like a sponge, soaking up every bit of knowledge and experience she could get her hands on. She'd watch videos of other teams, study their tactics, and analyze their strengths and weaknesses. She'd ask her coaches questions, eager to learn everything she could about the beautiful game.

It wasn't all grit and perseverance, though. Additionally, there were several belly laughs. After a win, the squad would celebrate with dance parties and pizza feasts, play practical jokes on one another, and sing ridiculous songs in the locker room. Their common goal of becoming World Cup champions brought them closer together as a family and a group of soccer fans.

As the tournament drew closer, the training intensified. It was like the final boss level in a video game, where everything they had learned was put to the test. They had to be prepared for anything, from surprise attacks to last-minute heroics.

The pressure was on, but Alex wasn't afraid. She knew she had put in the work, she trusted her teammates, and she believed in herself. She was ready to take on the world, one kick at a time.

Overcoming Injuries

Is a scraped knee anything you've ever experienced when running? That hurts! Well, isn't that painful? Just picture yourself hurting while participating in your favorite sport. On her way to become a soccer superstar, Alex experienced that more than time.

One day, while sprinting down the field, a fierce competitor like a hungry cheetah, Alex felt a sudden twinge in her ankle. It was like a tiny gremlin had jumped out and grabbed her foot. Turns out, she had sprained it. The pain was intense, like a thousand fire ants marching on her skin. But more than the pain, Alex felt a deep sadness. Would she be able to play in the upcoming big game? Would she let her team down?

Injuries are like those pesky speed bumps on a racetrack, slowing you down and sometimes forcing you to take a detour. For Alex, this meant sitting on the sidelines, watching her teammates practice and play while she rested and recovered. It was like being a hungry kid with their nose pressed against a bakery window, watching all the delicious treats they couldn't have.

Alex, nevertheless, was not the kind to wallow in misery. The woman was a soccer ninja, a fighter, and a warrior. Her injuries were nothing more than a jigsaw piece to the puzzle of her life. The recommendations of her physicians and physical therapists were like a map to her recovery, and she faithfully followed them.

Instead of sulking, Alex turned her injury into an opportunity. She used the time off to study the game, analyzing her own performance and learning from other players. She'd watch videos, read books, and even talk to other athletes who had overcome similar injuries.

Alex also focused on strengthening other parts of her body, like her arms and core. She did exercises that wouldn't put stress on her ankle, but would still help her stay in shape and maintain her fitness level. It was like building a secret weapon, ready to be unleashed when she returned to the field.

The road to recovery wasn't always smooth. There were days when Alex felt frustrated, discouraged, and even a little scared. She wondered if she would ever be the same player again, if she would ever be able to run, jump, and kick with the same power and agility.

Alex, though, possessed an unsung hero: an optimistic outlook. She was determined not to give in to pessimism. She chose to surround herself with positive, encouraging individuals who believed in her, concentrate on her objectives, and see herself performing again.

Her family, friends, and teammates rallied around her, offering encouragement, cheering her on, and reminding her of how strong and resilient she was. It was like a team huddle, with everyone coming together to lift Alex's spirits and help her through this tough time.

And slowly but surely, Alex started to heal. The pain in her ankle subsided, the swelling went down, and she was able to start moving around again. It was like a caterpillar emerging from its cocoon, ready to spread its wings and fly.

Alex started with light exercises, gradually increasing the intensity as her ankle grew stronger. She worked with her physical therapist to regain her range of motion and rebuild her muscle strength. It was like training for a marathon, one small step at a time.

2011 World Cup Debut

Think about this: On the largest soccer platform in the world, surrounded by an ovation, stood a young Alex Morgan, prepared to showcase her abilities to the world. With teams competing for the title from all around the world, the 2011 Women's World Cup was like a huge celebration. For Alex, it was an opportunity to fulfill a lifelong ambition of hers—

to play on the most prestigious platform in the world for her nation.

Being the youngest player on the team was like being the new kid at school, but Alex wasn't intimidated. She was excited, nervous, and bursting with energy, like a shaken-up soda can ready to explode. She knew she had to prove herself, to show that she belonged among the best players in the world.

The tournament was a whirlwind of emotions for Alex. She watched from the bench as her teammates battled it out in the early games, cheering them on with all her might. She soaked up the atmosphere, the chants of the crowd, the smell of the grass, the electric energy in the air. She was like a sponge, absorbing every detail, every experience, preparing herself for the moment she would step onto the field.

And that moment came sooner than she expected. In the semi-final match against France, Alex was called upon as a substitute. It was like a superhero getting the signal to spring into action. Her heart pounded with excitement as she ran onto the field, the roar of the crowd washing over her.

Alex didn't waste any time making an impact. With just minutes left in the game, she found herself with the ball at her feet, just outside the penalty box. She took a deep breath, channeled all her training and determination, and unleashed a rocket of a shot.

The ball soared through the air, past the outstretched arms of the goalkeeper, and nestled into the back of the net. The crowd erupted in cheers, her teammates rushed to embrace her, and Alex's face beamed with pure joy. She had scored her first World Cup goal, a moment she would never forget.

But it wasn't the end of Alex's heroic deeds. She made another halfway substitution in the championship match vs Japan. The United States needed a spark since they were behind. It was given by Alex.

She scored a crucial goal, tying the game and sending it into overtime. Then, in extra time, she delivered a perfect assist to her teammate, Abby Wambach, who headed the ball into the net for the winning goal.

It was a storybook ending, a dream come true for Alex and her teammates. They had won the silver medal, a testament to their hard work, dedication, and unwavering belief in themselves.

Alex's performance at the 2011 World Cup was a breakout moment, a sign of things to come. She had proven that she belonged among the elite, that she was a rising star in the world of women's soccer.

Alex faced a lot of challenges on her way to the World Cup, including injuries and setbacks. What are some challenges you've faced in your life? How did you overcome them?

Alex's 2011 World Cup debut was a dream come true. Have you ever achieved a goal you worked really hard for? How did it feel?

_____

_____

_____

_____

_____

_____

The World Cup is the biggest stage in soccer. What are some "big stages" or important events in your life? How do you prepare for them?

_____

_____

_____

_____

_____

What do you think it means to "never give up"? Can you think of a time when you didn't give up, even when things were difficult?

Alex had to train hard to prepare for the World Cup. What are some things you practice or train for to get better at something you enjoy?

Chapter 5: Olympic Glory

> *"Success is no accident. It is hard work, perseverance, learning, studying, sacrifice, and most of all, love of what you are doing or learning to do." - Pelé*

London 2012 Olympics

London was calling! Not just for the Queen and her corgis, but for the world's greatest athletes, ready to compete in the 2012 Summer Olympics. For Alex Morgan and the U.S. Women's National Team, it was a chance to chase another gold medal, a chance to show the world that they were still the queens of the pitch.

The Olympic Games are like a giant playground for athletes, but instead of swings and slides, there are stadiums and arenas filled with cheering fans. It's where dreams are made, records are broken, and legends are born. And for Alex, it was the chance to add another chapter to her already incredible story.

Stepping onto the field for the opening ceremony was like walking onto a movie set. The stadium was ablaze with lights, the air thrumming with excitement, and the athletes from all over the world marched in a colorful parade, waving to the crowd. Alex felt a surge of pride as she walked alongside her teammates, wearing the red, white, and blue of Team USA.

The Olympic tournament was a rollercoaster ride of emotions for Alex and her teammates. They faced tough opponents, battled through injuries, and weathered setbacks. But they never lost sight of their goal: to win gold.

Each game was like a mini-drama, filled with suspense, excitement, and nail-biting finishes. Alex played with her heart on her sleeve, running tirelessly, battling for every ball, and scoring crucial goals. She was like a spark plug, igniting her team's energy and inspiring them to play their best.

Playing Canada in the semi-finals was one of the tournament's most exciting moments. Time was of the essence as the game remained tied. Megan Rapinoe, Alex's teammate, passed the ball to her with an extra few seconds to go. With a powerful jump, she sent the ball soaring over the Canadian goalkeeper's outstretched arms after her head made contact with the ball.

The stadium erupted in cheers, the U.S. players mobbed Alex, and the dream of a gold medal was within reach. It was a moment of pure magic, a testament to Alex's skill, athleticism, and unwavering determination.

It was still early in the voyage. Rematching the World Cup final from the previous year, the last match versus Japan was soon to be played. It was an opportunity for atonement, to demonstrate their supremacy.

The game was full of intense back-and-forth play from both sides. The Japanese defense stood solid despite many scoring opportunities for Alex. It appeared like a penalty shootout was in the cards as time ran down.

However, Carli Lloyd, who was Alex's teammate, scored a goal in the dying minutes with a rocket shot from outside the penalty area. A quick shot by an American player beat the goaltender and put the Americans up 2-1.

The final whistle blew, and the U.S. Women's National Team had done it again. They were Olympic champions, their gold medals gleaming in the London sunlight. Alex and her teammates celebrated on the field, hugging each other, crying tears of joy, and waving to the ecstatic crowd.

It was a moment they would cherish forever, a testament to their teamwork, their resilience, and their unwavering belief in themselves.

Celebrating Victory

Winning the Olympic gold medal wasn't just about the game, the score, or even the shiny medal itself. It was like a giant party, a celebration of all the hard work, sweat, and tears that Alex and her teammates had poured into their journey. It was time to let loose, have some fun, and show the world how champions celebrate!

Picture the stadium filled with confetti, streamers falling from the sky, with the rousing chant of "We Are the Champions" resonating throughout the venue. When the final whistle sounded, that was only the beginning of the wild celebration. After another victory, the United States Women's National Team was prepared to celebrate like it was 1999!

First things first, the medal ceremony. It was like a scene from a fairy tale, with Alex and her teammates standing on the podium, the Olympic anthem playing, and the gold medals being placed around their necks. The medals were heavy, a symbol of all the blood, sweat, and tears they had shed to earn them. But they were also a symbol of pride, joy, and accomplishment.

As the American flag was raised and the national anthem played, Alex felt a surge of emotion. She looked around at her teammates, their faces beaming with pride, and she knew that this was a moment they would cherish forever. They had done it together, as a team, as a family.

But that wasn't the last act of merriment. The true celebration began once everyone returned to the locker room. The athletes blasted each other with champagne while dancing and singing. Seeing everyone having fun and reveling in their hard work was like something out of a music video.

Still, the changing area was the scene of more revelry. Returning to the Olympic Village, the squad was met with an overwhelming number of jubilant spectators. People were shouting, brandishing placards, and waving flags, making it look like a rock concert.

While high-fiving spectators, signing autographs, and posing for photos, the players completed a victory lap around the town. Millions of people all throughout the globe looked up to them as heroes and superstars. For all the athletes, it was a once in a lifetime, unbelievable opportunity.

However, joy and celebration were not the only goals of the event. Giving back and helping others build on their achievements were other important themes. As they went from hospital to school to community center, the group encouraged young people and shared a message of hope.

They shared their stories, their struggles, and their triumphs, showing others that anything is possible if you set your mind to it and work hard. They encouraged kids to chase their dreams, no matter how big or small, and to never give up on themselves.

The Olympic victory was a celebration of teamwork, dedication, and the unwavering spirit of the human will. It was a reminder that dreams can come true, that obstacles can be overcome, and that anything is possible when you believe in yourself and work together.

Alex and her team won the gold medal at the 2012 Olympics. Have you ever been part of a team or group that achieved something amazing together? How did it feel?

Alex scored a very important goal in the Olympics. Can you think of a time when you did something that helped your team or group succeed? What was it?

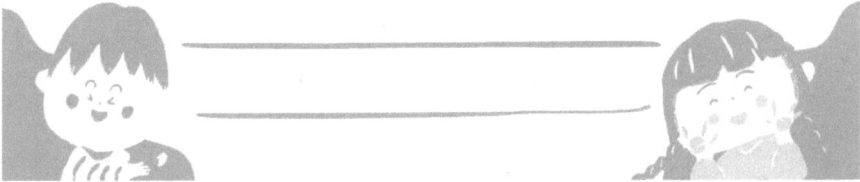

_____

_____

_____

_____

_____

_____

The Olympics are a special event where athletes from all over the world come together. What are some events or traditions that bring your family or community together?

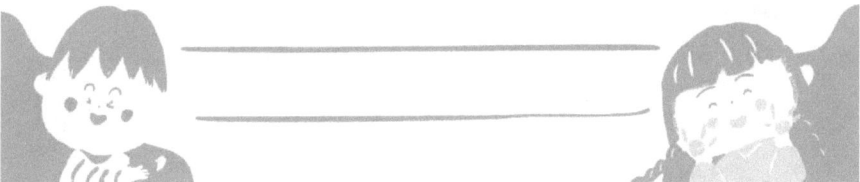

_____

_____

_____

_____

_____

_____

What do you think it means to celebrate a victory? How do you like to celebrate when you achieve a goal or do something well?

_____

_____

_____

_____

_____

_____

Alex felt proud to represent her country at the Olympics. What are some things you're proud of about yourself or your community?

_____

_____

_____

_____

_____

_____

Chapter 6: Becoming a Role Model

> *"Believe in yourself and all that you are. Know that there is something inside you that is greater than any obstacle." - Christian D. Larson*

Inspiring Young Athletes

Envision Alex Morgan, a genuine soccer prodigy, arriving to your school, carrying her cleats, prepared to engage in a game of soccer and divulge her strategies for achieving greatness. Impressive, isn't it? That is precisely the role she does for several young athletes globally. She is not only a participant; she serves as a source of motivation, an exemplar, a symbol of optimism for children who aspire to attain exceptional accomplishments.

Alex knows that being a professional athlete isn't just about scoring goals or winning trophies. It's about inspiring others, using your platform to make a difference, and showing kids that anything is possible if you set your mind to it and work hard.

When Alex visits schools and youth soccer camps, it's like a rock concert for aspiring athletes. The kids' faces light up with excitement as she shares stories from her own journey, talks about the challenges she's faced, and offers tips on how to improve their game.

But soccer prowess is only part of it. Having a good mindset, working together, and being persistent are all things that Alex advocates for. She reassures them that it's normal to learn from their errors and fall down sometimes. The important thing is to pick yourself up, reflect on what happened, and go on.

Alex's words are like magic spells, sparking a fire in the hearts of young athletes. She makes them believe in themselves, in their abilities, and in their dreams. She shows them that with hard work, dedication, and a whole lot of heart, they can achieve anything they set their minds to.

There is more to Alex's impact than meets the eye. She's also an inspiration to young women everywhere, showing them that athletic achievement is within reach. In doing so, she disproves gender norms and demonstrates that females can achieve the same level of physical prowess, academic achievement, and social success as guys.

When young girls see Alex on the field, scoring goals and celebrating victories, it gives them permission to dream big. It shows them that they can be anything they want to be, whether it's a soccer player, a doctor, a scientist, or anything else their hearts desire.

Alex's impact on young athletes is immeasurable. She inspires them to chase their dreams, to push their limits, and to never give up on themselves. She gives them hope, courage, and the confidence to believe in their own abilities.

But Alex isn't just inspiring young athletes; she's also empowering them. She teaches them to use their voices, to speak up for what they believe in, and to fight for equality. She shows them that they can make a difference in the world, both on and off the field.

Speaking Out for Equality

Alex Morgan is not only a superstar on the soccer field, but she also has a voice that echoes louder than a stadium full of cheering fans. It's a voice that speaks up for what's fair, what's right, and what's equal. Imagine a world where everyone, no matter their gender, gets the same opportunities to shine. That's the world Alex fights for, both on and off the field.

Think of it like a seesaw. On one side are the boys' soccer teams, and on the other side are the girls' teams. Sometimes, the seesaw isn't balanced. The boys' teams might get more resources, better facilities, or even more recognition. It's like the boys' side of the seesaw is weighed down with extra candy bars, making it harder for the girls to rise up.

But Alex Morgan isn't one to sit back and watch the seesaw stay tilted. She's like a strong gust of wind, pushing the girls' side up until it's perfectly balanced. She believes that girls deserve the same opportunities as boys, the same chance to play, to compete, and to achieve their dreams.

Alex uses her platform as a famous athlete to speak out about this issue. She talks to reporters, writes articles, and even meets with important people like politicians and business leaders. She explains that girls' soccer teams bring in just as much money as boys' teams, sometimes even more! Yet, they don't always get treated the same way.

Aside from soccer, Alex has other things on his mind. All sorts of issues including unequal treatment of girls and women are being brought up by her. Did you realize, for instance, that there are occupations where women earn less than males do for equivalent work? If you ate the same quantity of pizza, it would be like having a smaller piece! Alex isn't hesitant to voice her opinion that it's unfair.

Speaking out for equality isn't always easy. Some people might not like what Alex has to say. They might try to silence her or tell her to stick to soccer. But Alex is brave, and she won't back down. She knows that her voice is powerful, and she's going to use it to make a difference.

Alex's actions inspire other people, both young and old. She shows them that it's okay to stand up for what you believe in, even if it's hard. She teaches them that everyone deserves to be treated with respect and fairness, regardless of their gender.

Alex is like a role model, showing others how to use their voices to make a positive impact in the world. She encourages kids to speak up when they see something that isn't right, to stand up for their friends who are being treated unfairly, and to always fight for what they believe in.

Alex Morgan is a role model for many young athletes. Who are some of your role models? What qualities do you admire in them?

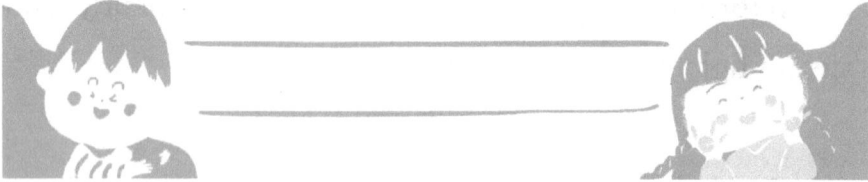

_____

_____

_____

_____

_____

_____

Alex uses her platform to speak out for equality. Have you ever spoken up for something you believe in, even if it was difficult? What was it?

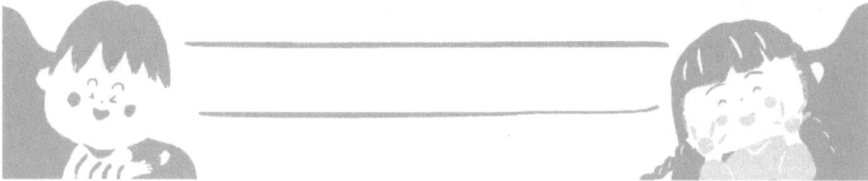

_____

_____

_____

_____

_____

Alex wants to inspire young athletes to chase their dreams. What are your dreams? What steps can you take to make them happen?

_____

_____

_____

_____

_____

_____

What do you think it means to be a good role model? What are some ways you can be a role model for others?

_____

_____

_____

_____

_____

Alex uses her voice to make a difference in the world. How can you use your voice to help others or make your community a better place?

Chapter 7: Balancing Family and Career

"Family is not an important thing, it's everything." - Michael J. Fox

Getting Married

Life is full of surprises, like finding a hidden treasure chest or winning a giant teddy bear at a carnival. And for Alex Morgan, one of the biggest surprises was finding love. It wasn't on a soccer field or during a training session; it was in a college classroom, where she met a guy named Servando Carrasco, who also happened to be a soccer player. Talk about a match made in heaven!

They were like two peas in a pod, both passionate about soccer, both driven to succeed, and both with hearts full of dreams. They bonded over their love for the game, their shared experiences as student-athletes, and their goofy sense of humor. They were each other's biggest fans, cheering each other on from the sidelines and celebrating each other's victories.

Their love story was like a fairy tale, but instead of castles and dragons, there were soccer balls and cleats. They'd go on romantic dates to the beach, watch movies under the stars, and even challenge each other to impromptu soccer matches in the park.

Their connection, though, was about more than simply having fun. Injuries, failures, and the stresses of their professions weren't enough to deter them from being there for one other. When one of them needed someone to talk to, someone to weep on, or someone to cheer them on, the other would be there for them.

As their love grew stronger, they realized that they wanted to spend the rest of their lives together. So, on New Year's Eve, Servando surprised Alex with a romantic proposal. It was like a scene from a movie, with fireworks exploding in the background and tears of joy streaming down Alex's face.

Of course, she said yes! They were both so excited to start this new chapter of their lives together, to build a family, and to continue chasing their dreams, hand in hand.

Planning a wedding is like organizing a giant puzzle, with all the pieces needing to fit together perfectly. Alex and Servando had to find the perfect venue, the perfect dress, the perfect flowers, and the perfect cake. It was like a scavenger hunt, but instead of searching for hidden clues, they were searching for the perfect elements to make their wedding day unforgettable.

The love they shared, though, was more vital than any amount of preparation or planning. Alex and Servando exchanged vows on their wedding day, vowing to love, honor, and cherish one other forever in the presence of their loved ones. Laughter, tears, and touching moments abound in the lovely wedding.

Their wedding wasn't just a party; it was a celebration of their love, their commitment, and their shared journey. It was a day they would cherish forever, a reminder of the special bond they shared and the exciting future they were building together.

Getting married didn't change Alex's focus on her soccer career. In fact, it made her even more determined to succeed. She knew that she had the love and support of her husband, and that gave her the strength and confidence to chase her dreams with even more passion and determination.

Their love story is a reminder that even the busiest people can find time for love, that even the most ambitious dreams can be achieved with the support of a loving partner, and that with hard work, dedication, and a whole lot of love, anything is possible.

Becoming a Mom

Riding a roller coaster and discovering a secret rainforest are just two examples of the thrilling adventures that await you in life. However, being a mother was one of the most incredible journeys for Alex Morgan. With the addition of a small, cute buddy, the game took on a whole new dimension.

Imagine a little bundle of joy, with chubby cheeks, tiny fingers, and a smile that could melt your heart. That's what Alex and Servando's daughter, Charlie, was like. She was their little miracle, a tiny human being who brought so much love and happiness into their lives.

Becoming a mom was like a whole new training camp for Alex. She had to learn new skills, like changing diapers, feeding a tiny baby, and soothing a crying infant. It was like a whole new sport, with challenges and rewards unlike any she had experienced on the soccer field.

Alex, though, was ready for anything. She devoted herself fully to parenting, just as she had to soccer. She did her research, talked to professionals, and sought out the opinions of other mothers. Finding a happy medium between her soccer career and her newfound obligations allowed her to support her family well.

Being a mom wasn't always easy. There were sleepless nights, endless diaper changes, and moments of frustration. But there were also moments of pure joy, like the first time Charlie smiled, the first time she giggled, and the first time she called Alex "mama."

Motherhood changed Alex in many ways. It made her more patient, more compassionate, and more appreciative of the little things in life. It taught her the true meaning of unconditional love, the kind of love that knows no bounds and that lasts a lifetime.

Despite becoming a mother, Alex's passion for soccer remained unmatched. Actually, it just served to strengthen her will to achieve her goals. She hoped to prove to Charlie that he can achieve his dreams if he puts his mind to it. To encourage her daughter to follow her passions and persevere through tough times, she aspired to provide a good example.

So, Alex continued to train, to play, and to compete. She juggled her soccer career with her new responsibilities as a mom, finding a way to make it all work. It wasn't always easy, but Alex was determined to show the world that you can be a mom and a successful athlete at the same time.

Being a mom didn't just change Alex; it also changed her perspective on soccer. She realized that it wasn't just a game; it was a platform, a way to inspire and empower others. She wanted to use her voice and her influence to make a positive impact in the world, not just for herself, but for her daughter and for all the other little girls who dreamed of playing soccer.

Alex's journey as a mom is a testament to the strength and resilience of women. It shows that motherhood doesn't have to be a limitation; it can be a source of strength, inspiration, and motivation. It's a reminder that with love, support, and determination, anything is possible.

Juggling Responsibilities

Imagine being a superhero, juggling a million different things at once. You have to save the world, fight off villains, and still find time to eat your veggies. That's kind of what it was like for Alex Morgan as she became a mom while continuing to play professional soccer. It was like a super-charged game of tag, with baby bottles, soccer balls, and to-do lists flying everywhere!

First, there was Charlie, her adorable little daughter who needed cuddles, diaper changes, and lots of love. Alex wanted to be the best mom she could be, the kind of mom who could read bedtime stories, build pillow forts, and chase butterflies in the park.

Soccer, though, was always there; it was her ideal career and a passion of hers. As an athlete, Alex aspired to continue playing, score goals, win titles, and motivate young athletes all across the globe. Just because she became a mother didn't mean she wanted to abandon her work.

So, Alex became a master juggler, balancing her roles as a mom and a professional athlete. It was like a high-wire act, with no safety net, but Alex was determined to make it work. She created a schedule that allowed her to spend quality time with Charlie while still training and playing soccer.

Some days were easier than others. There were times when Alex felt overwhelmed, like a clown juggling too many bowling pins at once. She'd have to wake up early for practice, then rush home to feed Charlie, then squeeze in a nap before heading back to the field for another training session.

The people who believed in Alex, nevertheless, were her hidden weapon. In times of need, her husband Servando would be the one to step in and help, whether it was changing a diaper or just listening to her vent. A lot of her friends and relatives were also very encouraging, volunteering to watch Charlie while Alex trained.

Even her teammates and coaches were understanding, cheering her on and helping her find ways to balance her commitments. They knew that Alex was more than just a soccer player; she was a mom, a wife, and a role model for young women everywhere.

With their help, Alex was able to continue playing soccer at the highest level, even while raising a young child. She traveled the world with her team, competed in major tournaments, and continued to score goals and win championships.

On the other hand, she was very careful to spend quality time with Charlie. She would take her kid to games and practices so she could feel the thrill of the sport. Prior to her slumber, she would lullaby sing to her, give her a bedtime story, and instruct her in the art of backyard soccer.

Alex's ability to juggle her responsibilities was a testament to her strength, her determination, and her unwavering love for her family and her sport. She proved that you can be a mom and a successful athlete at the same time, that you can chase your dreams and still be there for your loved ones.

Alex had to learn to balance her career as a soccer player with her new role as a mom. Have you ever had to balance different things you love, like school and hobbies? How did you do it?

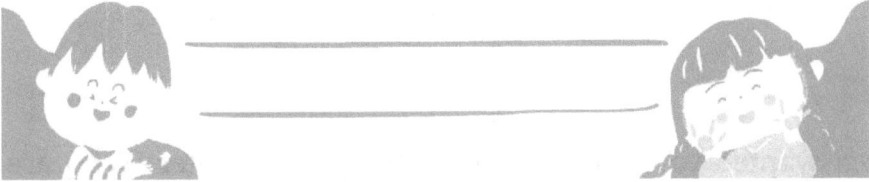

_____

_____

_____

_____

_____

_____

Alex and Servando worked as a team to take care of their daughter. Who are the people in your family who work together as a team? What do they do together?

_____

_____

_____

_____

_____

_____

Becoming a mom was a big change for Alex. What are some changes you've experienced in your life? How did you adapt to them?

_____

_____

_____

_____

_____

Alex wanted to be a role model for her daughter. Who are some people in your life who inspire you? What qualities do you admire in them?

_____

_____

_____

_____

_____

Juggling responsibilities can be tricky! What are some things you juggle in your own life, like school, chores, or activities?

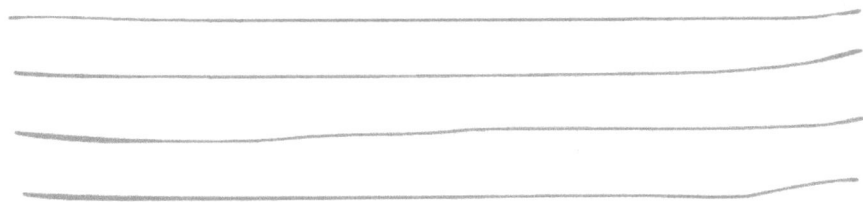

Chapter 8: Leading the Team

> *"The greatest glory in living lies not in never falling, but in rising every time we fall." - Nelson Mandela*

Captain Morgan

Picture yourself with a treasure map in one hand, a crew of enthusiastic sailors eager to follow your direction, and the keys to a pirate ship in the other. That's about how Alex Morgan felt when the United States Women's National Team appointed her co-captain. Being named captain of her squad was more than simply a privilege; it was an opportunity for greatness.

Being a captain isn't just about wearing a fancy armband. It's about being a leader, a role model, and an inspiration to your teammates. It's about setting the tone, lifting spirits, and motivating everyone to play their best.

Alex was born to be a leader. She had a natural charisma, a way of rallying the troops and making everyone feel like they were part of something special. She was like a cheerleader, a coach, and a friend all rolled into one.

On the field, Alex led by example. She played with her heart on her sleeve, never giving up, always pushing herself to be better. She was a vocal leader, communicating with her teammates, directing their movements, and encouraging them to keep fighting.

There was more to Alex than being a dictator who screamed out commands and wanted immediate action. Aside from being a friend, she was someone you could lean on in times of need and talk to about anything. Every one of her colleagues was more than a mere athlete to her; they were real people with feelings, problems, and aspirations.

Off the field, Alex was just as important. She organized team-building activities, like karaoke nights and scavenger hunts. She made sure everyone felt included and valued, fostering a sense of camaraderie and trust.

She also took on a mentorship role, guiding younger players and helping them navigate the challenges of being a professional athlete. She shared her experiences, offered advice, and encouraged them to chase their dreams.
Being a captain wasn't always easy. There were times when Alex had to make tough decisions, like benching a player or addressing a conflict within the team. But she always did what

she thought was best for the team, even if it meant making unpopular choices.

She also had to deal with the pressure of being a leader. Everyone looked up to her, expected her to be perfect, to always have the answers. But Alex was human, just like everyone else. She made mistakes, had doubts, and sometimes felt overwhelmed.

Those things, nonetheless, never came to define her. She wanted to be the greatest captain she could be at all times, learning from her mistakes and growing from her experiences. Being genuine, caring, and motivating were more important than being flawless, as she understood.

Under Alex's leadership, the U.S. Women's National Team thrived. They won championships, set records, and became a dominant force in the world of women's soccer. But more than that, they became a family, a team of sisters who supported each other, challenged each other, and celebrated each other's successes.

Building Team Spirit

A soccer team isn't just a bunch of players wearing the same jersey; it's like a band of superheroes, each with their own unique powers, working together to save the day. And just like any superhero team, they need to have strong team spirit, a bond that unites them and makes them stronger than the sum of their parts.

Alex Morgan, as co-captain of the U.S. Women's National Team, knew that building team spirit was just as important as practicing drills or perfecting strategies. She knew that a team that plays together, stays together, and wins together.

So, Alex became the team's cheerleader-in-chief, the one who always had a smile on her face, a pep talk in her pocket, and a knack for bringing people together. She organized team-building activities that were as fun as they were effective, like karaoke nights where players belted out their favorite tunes, scavenger hunts that sent them on wild goose chases around the city, and even impromptu dance parties in the locker room.

Alex understood that team spirit wasn't just about having fun; it was about creating a sense of trust, camaraderie, and mutual respect. She encouraged her teammates to get to know each other on a deeper level, to share their stories, their hopes, and their dreams. She organized team dinners, movie nights, and even volunteer activities, where the players could bond outside of the soccer field.

But Alex was also aware that the team's camaraderie needed to carry over onto the field. She was a role model for the rest of the team because she never stopped working, never stopped giving 110%, and never placed herself last. She reveled in her teammates' victories, was there for them when they were down, and never stopped telling them that they were better off as a team.

She encouraged open communication, creating a safe space where players could express their opinions, share their ideas, and work together to solve problems. She fostered a culture of trust, where players felt comfortable taking risks, trying new things, and pushing their limits.

One of her favorite ways to build team spirit was through music. She'd create playlists for the team bus, blasting upbeat tunes that got everyone pumped up for the game. She'd even lead impromptu sing-alongs, with players belting out their favorite lyrics at the top of their lungs.

But there were some serious moments as well. In addition, Alex was aware that it was only through hardship that true team spirit could be developed. She was the one who rallied the team whenever they encountered difficulties by pointing out their shared values, their ambitions, and their capabilities.

She'd give inspiring speeches, share motivational quotes, and even write personal notes to her teammates, reminding them of how much they meant to her and to the team. She was like a coach, a cheerleader, and a therapist all rolled into one. Under Alex's leadership, the U.S. Women's National Team became more than just a team; they became a family, a sisterhood, a band of warriors who fought together, celebrated together, and grew together. They learned that true strength comes from unity, that trust is the foundation of success, and that together, they could achieve anything.

Alex's efforts to build team spirit paid off in spades. The team became a dominant force in the world of women's soccer, winning championships, setting records, and inspiring millions of fans around the globe. But more than that, they created a legacy of teamwork, camaraderie, and sportsmanship that would continue to inspire generations to come.

Facing Challenges Together

Think of a team of superheroes that are united in their mission to rescue the planet. Along the way, they encounter nefarious characters, catastrophic events, and even a rare huge robot. As a team, though, they are able to conquer any challenge that comes their way. The United States Women's National Soccer Team was no different; captain Alex Morgan never wavered from the wheel.

No team, even a team of superstars, is immune to challenges. There are going to be tough games, injuries, setbacks, and disagreements. But what separates a good team from a great team is how they face those challenges together.

Alex knew that a team is only as strong as its weakest link. So, she made it her mission to create a culture of support, encouragement, and resilience within the team. She wanted her teammates to know that they weren't alone, that they had each other's backs, no matter what.

When a teammate was struggling, Alex was the first one to offer a helping hand. She'd listen patiently, offer words of encouragement, and remind them of their strengths and abilities. She'd organize extra training sessions, help them analyze their performance, and find ways for them to improve.

When the team faced a tough opponent, Alex would rally the troops, reminding them of their past successes and their potential for greatness. She'd give inspiring speeches, share motivational quotes, and even create silly chants to boost morale. She was like a cheerleader, a coach, and a therapist all rolled into one.

One of the biggest challenges the team faced was dealing with injuries. Soccer is a physical sport, and injuries are an inevitable part of the game. But Alex knew that losing a player to injury could be devastating, both for the individual and for the team.

So, when a teammate got hurt, Alex made sure they felt supported and loved. She'd visit them in the hospital, send them get-well cards, and keep them updated on the team's progress. She'd also make sure that the injured player had a plan for recovery, working with them to set goals and track their progress.

Another challenge the team faced was dealing with criticism and negativity from the outside world. Some people doubted their abilities, questioned their motives, or even criticized their appearance. It was like a bunch of grumpy trolls trying to rain on their parade.

But Alex taught her teammates to rise above the negativity. She reminded them of their own worth, their own accomplishments, and their own dreams. She encouraged them to focus on the positive, to block out the haters, and to keep playing with passion and joy.

She also led by example, always maintaining a positive attitude and never letting the negativity get to her. She was like a shield, protecting her teammates from the slings and arrows of outrageous fortune.

Through it all, Alex remained a source of strength, inspiration, and unwavering optimism. She taught her teammates that challenges are not roadblocks; they are opportunities for growth, learning, and coming together as a team.

Alex was chosen as captain of her team. Have you ever been a leader in a group or activity? What did it feel like? What were your responsibilities?

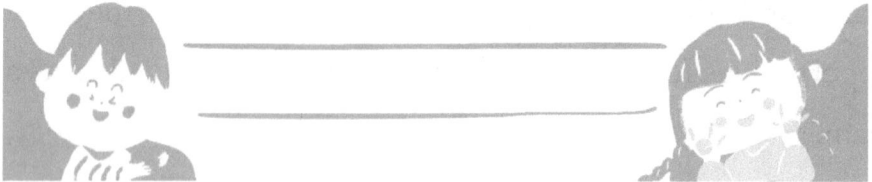

_____

_____

_____

_____

_____

_____

Building team spirit is important for success. How do you help create a positive and fun atmosphere when you're working with others?

_____

_____

_____

_____

_____

_____

Alex faced challenges as a captain. Have you ever had to make tough decisions or deal with disagreements when working with others? How did you handle it?

_____

_____

_____

_____

_____

_____

What qualities do you think make a good leader? Are you a leader in any way in your life?

_____

_____

_____

_____

_____

Alex always tried to encourage and support her teammates. How can you be a good friend and teammate to others?

Chapter 9: World Cup Champions Again!

> *"Fight for the things that you care about, but do it in a way that will lead others to join you."*
> *- Ruth Bader Ginsburg*

2019 World Cup Journey

The thrill of the 2019 Women's World Cup was electric, buzzing through the air like a swarm of excited bees. It was a global stage set for the best female soccer players to showcase their skills, passion, and unwavering determination. The journey was not just about defending their title for Alex Morgan and the U.S. Women's National Team; it was about etching their names into the annals of soccer history.

The road to France, where the World Cup was held, was a mosaic of intense training sessions, exhilarating victories, and the occasional tough loss that served as a learning curve. The team faced a gauntlet of friendly matches against formidable opponents from around the world. Each game was a unique challenge, a chance to fine-tune their tactics, test their resilience, and build their confidence.

Alex Morgan, the team's co-captain, was a beacon of inspiration on and off the field. Her leadership skills were as sharp as her goal-scoring instincts. She motivated her teammates, instilled a sense of unity that was unbreakable, and set a standard for performance that was nothing short of exceptional.

The opening match against Thailand was a spectacle to behold, a testament to the team's dominance. Alex Morgan made history by scoring five goals, an unprecedented feat in the tournament's history. It was a dazzling display of skill, precision, and unwavering determination that left the world in awe. Her teammates rallied around her, their spirits soaring high with each goal, their bond strengthening with every shared celebration.

The road to triumph, nevertheless, was not without its share of difficulties. Match after match was a brutal examination of their skills against strong opponents like England, France, and Spain. Feelings of impending doom, moments of exasperation, and wasted chances all chipped away at their self-assurance. Their hidden weapon, though, was the team's resiliency. After each setback, they analyzed what went wrong, adjusted their strategy to counter their opponents' moves, and eventually came out on top.

The quarter-final against France was a pivotal moment, a clash of two soccer powerhouses. It was a tense match, with both teams vying fiercely for a spot in the semi-finals. Alex Morgan, with her signature blend of agility and precision, scored the decisive goal, a perfectly placed header that ignited the U.S. fans and sent a wave of euphoria through the stadium. The victory was a hard-fought one, a testament to the team's grit, determination, and unwavering belief in their collective strength.

The semi-final against England was equally thrilling, a battle of wills, a clash of titans. Alex Morgan, once again, rose to the occasion, scoring the winning goal with a display of athleticism and tactical brilliance that secured the team's place in the final.

The final against the Netherlands was a rematch of the 2015 final, a chance for both teams to write a new chapter in their rivalry. The atmosphere was electric, the tension so thick you could almost taste it. The U.S. team, led by the indomitable Alex Morgan, played with a fiery passion and unwavering focus. They dominated the game, their passing crisp and precise, their defense impenetrable. The Dutch team fought valiantly, but the Americans were unstoppable.

The final whistle blew, and the U.S. Women's National Team etched their names in history, becoming back-to-back World Cup champions. The stadium erupted in a symphony of cheers, tears of joy streamed down the players' faces, and the American flag danced proudly in the French breeze. It was a moment of pure elation, a culmination of years of tireless effort, unwavering dedication, and an unyielding belief in their collective destiny.

Alex and her team won the World Cup not just once, but twice! Have you ever worked really hard for something and achieved it more than once? What was it, and how did it feel?

The team's journey to the 2019 World Cup was filled with challenges. What are some challenges you have faced while trying to reach a goal? How did you overcome them?

Alex and her teammates made history with their back-to-back wins. Can you think of a time when you or someone you know made history or achieved something amazing?

The World Cup is a global event. What are some other global events or celebrations that you know about? What makes them special?

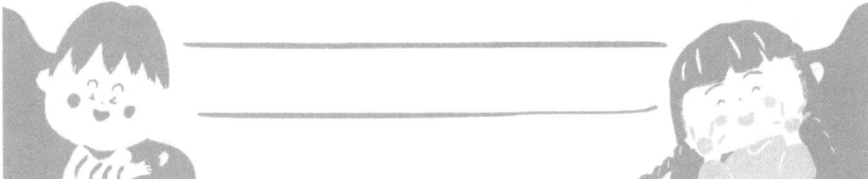

What do you think it means to be a champion? Do you think being a champion is only about winning, or are there other important aspects?

_____

_____

_____

_____

_____

_____

Chapter 10: Overcoming Adversity

The Pandemic's Impact

You might remember or would have heard about a giant pause button pressed on the world in the year 2020. Sports, concerts, and even going to school suddenly stop! That's exactly what happened when a pesky virus called COVID-19 showed up, throwing a wrench in everyone's plans, including Alex Morgan's.

For Alex, it was like someone had stolen her soccer ball and hidden it away. She couldn't practice with her teammates, couldn't play in front of cheering crowds, couldn't do what she loved most. It was a bummer, like a rainy day that wouldn't end.

But even a little sickness couldn't stop Alex. A soccer ninja, a champion, and a fighter—that was her! Like a chameleon that changes its color to fit in, she chose to adapt and overcome.

Instead of practicing on a field with her teammates, Alex transformed her living room into a mini gym. She did squats, lunges, and push-ups, using her furniture as makeshift exercise equipment. She even had her husband, Servando, act as her personal trainer, putting her through the paces and cheering her on.

When she wasn't working out, Alex found other ways to stay connected to the game she loved. She watched old soccer matches, studied the strategies of other teams, and even practiced her juggling skills in the backyard. She was like a detective, searching for clues to improve her game even when she couldn't play.

Changing up one's workout regimen wasn't the only challenge posed by the epidemic. Keeping oneself well and safe was also a major concern. Alex was very careful, taking measures such as washing her hands often, avoiding close contact with others, and wearing a mask. She placed equal value on safeguarding her family and herself as she did on scoring goals.

During this time, Alex also became a mom. It was a joyful time, but also a challenging one. Taking care of a newborn baby during a pandemic was like playing a video game on the hardest level, with unexpected obstacles and challenges popping up at every turn.

Despite this, Alex stepped up to the challenge, maintaining her dedication to health and fitness while adjusting to her new role as a mother. Even though she had to squeeze in training and workouts, she managed to keep her daughter Charlie occupied in inventive ways. While juggling diapers, soccer balls, and baby bottles, Alex looked like he was performing a circus show.

Although everything was happening, Alex kept her eye on the prize. Even if the epidemic was going to continue forever, she was still planning to be fully prepared for the return of soccer. She never stopped studying and training for her return to the international stage.

The pandemic was a tough time for everyone, but Alex used it as an opportunity to grow, both as an athlete and as a person. She learned to adapt, to improvise, and to appreciate the simple things in life. She discovered the importance of family, the value of staying connected to loved ones, and the power of hope.

Staying Motivated

Just picture your beloved playground all of a sudden locked up, with the swings and slides covered with warning tape. When the epidemic put a stop to all activities, Alex felt the same way. Attempting to construct a sandcastle in the absence of sand was an arduous task! But Alex's unbreakable spirit was her hidden weapon!

Alex knew that staying motivated was like keeping a fire burning. It needed fuel, a spark, and a whole lot of air to keep it going. So, she became her own personal cheerleader, pumping herself up with positive self-talk and setting mini-goals to keep her on track.

Every day, Alex would wake up with a mantra, a little saying that would get her fired up and ready to tackle whatever the day threw her way. It was like a secret code, a reminder of her strength and determination. "I am a champion," she'd say to herself, "I can do this!"

Alex also knew the power of setting small, achievable goals. It was like climbing a mountain, one step at a time. Instead of focusing on the big picture, like winning the World Cup, she'd set daily goals, like practicing a new skill or running a certain distance. It was like earning badges in a video game, each one a small victory that fueled her motivation.

One of Alex's favorite ways to stay motivated was to connect with her teammates virtually. They'd have video chats, online workouts, and even virtual dance parties! It was like a secret club, a place where they could laugh, share stories, and remind each other of their goals.

Alex also found inspiration in other athletes who had overcome challenges. She'd read their stories, watch their videos, and remind herself that anything is possible with hard work and dedication. It was like having a whole team of virtual coaches cheering her on from afar.

But it took more than mental tenacity to keep going. Alex was similarly aware of the need of tending to her physical health. She rested and rejuvenated herself by eating well, getting adequate sleep, and doing things she enjoyed. It felt like refueling a racing engine with high-octane fuel to get it ready for the next race.

Alex also found creative ways to stay active and engaged. She'd play soccer with her daughter in the backyard, go for hikes with her husband, and even try new sports, like tennis and pickleball. It was like a playground for adults, a way to have fun and stay fit at the same time.

Throughout the pandemic, Alex's positive attitude and unwavering determination were an inspiration to others. She showed that even when things get tough, it's possible to stay motivated, to keep chasing your dreams, and to find joy in the little things.

The fact that they're all facing this together was another point she said. No matter how far away they are geographically, they can always lean on one other, cheer each other on, and discover methods to remain connected. It resounds like a global jubilation, assuring them of hope that persists through thick and thin.

Returning to the Field

After what felt like a lifetime of waiting, the moment had finally arrived. The soccer fields were open again, the roar of the crowd echoed in the distance, and Alex Morgan was ready to make her triumphant return. It was like a superhero emerging from a secret lair, ready to save the day.

It wasn't as easy as putting on her soccer shoes and heading out to the field, though. The game had changed slightly while she was away, and months of preparation had worn her down. It was like going back to a beloved playground after an extended absence, only to discover that the swings had been raised and the monkey bars had been spaced out somewhat.

The first few practices were a whirlwind of emotions. There was excitement, anticipation, and a touch of nervousness. Alex was like a race car driver revving her engine, eager to test her skills on the track again. But there was also a sense of unfamiliarity, like trying to dance to a new rhythm.

The game had changed, and so had Alex. She was a mother now, with a whole new set of responsibilities and priorities. But her love for soccer hadn't diminished; in fact, it had grown even stronger. It was the fire that fueled her determination, the spark that ignited her passion.

Stepping onto the field for the first time was like a nostalgic homecoming, a joyous reunion with a dear friend from the past. The aroma of the grass, the tactile sensation of the ball on her feet, the auditory impact of her cleats striking the turf

- it was all incredibly familiar, yet noticeably distinct. It was reminiscent of a childhood recollection, but with a renewed admiration for the small details.

Alex's first game back was a whirlwind of emotions. There was the adrenaline rush of stepping onto the field, the roar of the crowd, and the nerves that tingled in her stomach. But there was also a sense of joy, a feeling of pure happiness that she was back where she belonged.

It wasn't a perfect game. Alex missed a few shots, made a few bad passes, and struggled to find her rhythm. But she didn't let that discourage her. She knew it would take time to get back into the swing of things, to regain her old form and adapt to the new challenges.

Every game was a learning experience, a chance to test her skills, her endurance, and her mental toughness. Alex watched hours of game footage, analyzing her performance and identifying areas where she could improve. She sought feedback from her coaches and teammates, eager to learn from their expertise.

And slowly but surely, Alex started to find her groove. Her touch on the ball became sharper, her passes more accurate, and her shots more powerful. It was like a rusty engine finally kicking into gear, the wheels turning smoothly, the pistons firing in perfect harmony.

With each game, Alex's confidence grew. She rediscovered her love for the game, her passion for competition, and her desire to be the best. She was like a phoenix rising from the ashes, stronger, wiser, and more determined than ever before.

The pandemic caused many changes in Alex's life. Have you ever experienced unexpected changes or challenges in your life? What were they?

Alex had to find new ways to stay motivated and active during the pandemic. What are some things you do to stay motivated when things get tough?

_____

_____

_____

_____

_____

_____

Even though it was difficult, Alex found ways to stay connected to soccer during the pandemic. Have you ever found creative ways to do something you love, even when it wasn't easy? What did you do?

_____

_____

_____

_____

_____

Returning to the field after a long break was a challenge for Alex. Have you ever had to start something again after a break? How did it feel?

_____

_____

_____

_____

_____

_____

Alex learned a lot about herself during the pandemic. What are some things you've learned about yourself during challenging times?

_____

_____

_____

_____

_____

_____

Chapter 11: Fighting for Equal Pay

> *"Don't just aspire to make a living. Aspire to make a difference." - Denzel Washington*

The Gender Pay Gap in Soccer

Imagine you and a pal selling lemonade on a hot summer day. You both labor hard, squeezing lemons, adding sugar, and serving cups of cool lemonade to thirsty clients. When it comes time to share your earnings, your friend receives a larger amount of coins than you. How would that make you feel?

That's kind of how Alex Morgan and her teammates felt when they discovered the gender pay gap in soccer. It means that even though they worked just as hard as the men's team, won just as many games, and brought in just as much money, they were getting paid less. It was like getting a smaller scoop of ice cream even though you ordered the same size as your friend!

This unfairness didn't sit well with Alex. She knew that she and her teammates deserved to be paid equally, just like anyone else who works hard and does their job well. It was like a puzzle piece that didn't fit, a sour note in a beautiful song.

The pay gap wasn't just about money; it was about respect, fairness, and equality. It was about recognizing the hard work and dedication of female athletes and valuing their contributions to the sport.

Alex wasn't one to sit back and accept this injustice. She was a fighter, a champion, a voice for those who couldn't speak up for themselves. She decided to take a stand, to use her platform as a famous athlete to raise awareness about the pay gap and fight for change.

She joined forces with her teammates, forming a united front. They talked to the media, wrote letters to officials, and even filed a lawsuit against the U.S. Soccer Federation. It was like a team huddle, but instead of planning their next play, they were strategizing how to tackle the issue of unequal pay.

Their struggle was tough. There were hindrances, adversities, and instances of uncertainty. However, Alex and her teammates persevered unwaveringly. They were aware that they were aligned with the correct side of history, engaged in a battle for a cause greater than their own selves.

They were like a team of superheroes, each with their own unique powers, working together to defeat a common enemy: inequality. Alex was the leader, the one who rallied the troops, gave inspiring speeches, and kept everyone focused on the goal.

Their fight for equal pay inspired people all over the world. Other female athletes spoke out in support, fans started petitions, and even politicians took notice. It was like a wave of change, sweeping across the globe, demanding fairness and equality for all.

The battle for equal pay wasn't just about soccer; it was about empowering women and girls everywhere. It was about showing them that they deserve to be treated with respect, that their voices matter, and that they can achieve anything they set their minds to.

Alex and her teammates didn't just play soccer; they made history. They showed the world that women athletes are just as valuable, just as skilled, and just as deserving of fair pay as their male counterparts. They proved that even the biggest giants can be defeated when people come together and fight for what's right.

Leading the Charge for Change

Alex wasn't afraid to use her platform as a famous athlete to speak out against the pay gap. She was like a megaphone, amplifying the voices of her teammates and all the other female athletes who were tired of being treated as second-class citizens. She used her interviews, social media posts, and public appearances to raise awareness about the issue and rally support for their cause.

It wasn't just about talking the talk; Alex also walked the walk. She and her teammates filed a lawsuit against the U.S. Soccer Federation, demanding equal pay and working conditions. It was a bold move, a risky move, but it was a necessary one.

The lawsuit was like a David vs. Goliath battle, with a group of determined women athletes taking on a powerful organization. But Alex and her teammates weren't intimidated. They were fueled by their passion for the game, their belief in equality, and their unwavering determination to make a difference.

Alex became the face of the fight for equal pay. She gave interviews on national television, spoke at rallies and conferences, and used her social media platform to reach millions of people. She was like a spokesperson for justice, explaining the issue in a way that everyone could understand.

Alex, however, was more than simply a speaker; she was also a strategist who collaborated with her colleagues and attorneys to formulate a strategy for the team's victory. To be ready for a long and tough battle, they gathered evidence, developed their arguments, and so on.

The court dispute resembled a marathon rather than a sprint. It required several years of diligent effort, commitment, and unwavering determination. There were obstacles, letdowns, and instances of uncertainty. However, Alex and her teammates persevered relentlessly. They were aware that they were battling for a cause greater than their own, one that would have a positive impact on future generations of female athletes.

Ultimately, their diligent efforts yielded positive results. In 2022, the U.S. Women's National Team achieved a significant resolution with the U.S. Soccer Federation, ensuring that the women's and men's national teams will receive equal compensation. It was a significant triumph, demonstrating the effectiveness of united efforts and the bravery of a small group who defended their convictions.

Alex Morgan's leadership in the fight for equal pay was a game-changer, not just for soccer, but for women's sports as a whole. She showed that female athletes are just as valuable, just as skilled, and just as deserving of respect and compensation as their male counterparts.

Her actions inspired a new generation of athletes to speak up, to demand change, and to never settle for anything less than equality. She showed that even the most powerful organizations can be challenged, and that even the biggest battles can be won when people unite for a common cause.

A Landmark Agreement

The fight for equal pay was like a long, intense soccer match, with both sides battling fiercely for victory. But after years of struggle, hard work, and unwavering determination, the whistle finally blew, and a landmark agreement was reached. It was like a referee raising their arms to signal a goal, a victory not just for Alex Morgan and her teammates, but for female athletes everywhere.

Imagine a giant puzzle finally coming together, all the pieces fitting perfectly into place. That's what it felt like when the U.S. Soccer Federation agreed to pay the women's and men's national teams equally. It was a moment of triumph, a testament to the power of perseverance and the importance of fighting for what's right.

The agreement wasn't just about money; it was about respect, recognition, and equality. It was about acknowledging the value and contributions of female athletes and ensuring that they were treated with the same fairness and dignity as their male counterparts.

It was like a giant leap forward, a victory not just for soccer, but for women's sports as a whole. It sent a message to the world that women athletes are just as skilled, just as dedicated, and just as deserving of fair compensation as men.

The news of the agreement spread like wildfire, igniting celebrations across the country and around the world. It was like a wave of joy, washing over everyone who had supported the fight for equal pay. Fans cheered, athletes rejoiced, and young girls everywhere saw a brighter future for themselves in sports.

The victory was a testament to the power of teamwork, the importance of standing up for what you believe in, and the unwavering spirit of the human will. It showed that even the biggest battles can be won when people unite for a common cause.

The agreement also opened doors for future generations of female athletes. It created a more level playing field, where girls and women could pursue their dreams without fear of discrimination or unequal treatment. It was like a key unlocking a treasure chest of opportunities, allowing female athletes to shine and reach their full potential.

Nonetheless, the struggle for parity persisted. Fair and equitable treatment of female athletes across all sports was still an area that needed improvement. However, the historic deal was a positive development, a triumph that would encourage and enable female athletes for a long time.

Alex Morgan and her teammates had shown the world that change is possible, that even the most powerful institutions can be challenged, and that when people come together and fight for what's right, anything is possible.

Their story is a reminder that dreams can come true, that obstacles can be overcome, and that even the smallest voices can make a big difference. It's a message of hope, inspiration, and empowerment, a reminder that we all have the power to make a difference in the world.

Alex and her teammates fought for equal pay in soccer. Have you ever felt something wasn't fair in a game, at school, or with your friends? What did you do about it?

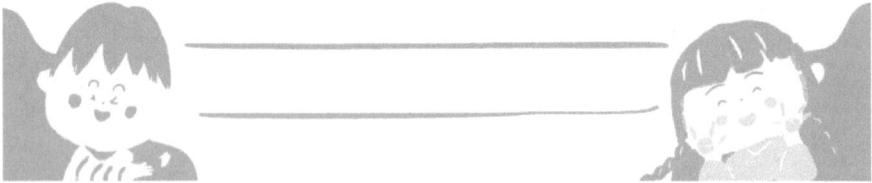

The women's soccer team was paid less than the men's team even though they worked just as hard and were just as successful. Can you think of any other examples where people aren't treated fairly because of their gender?

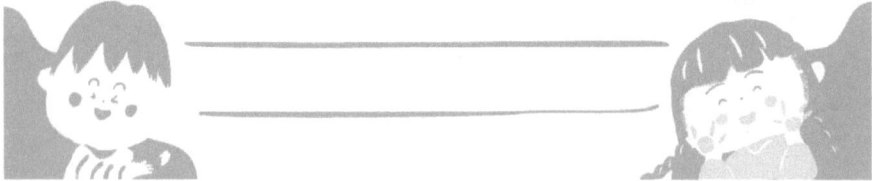

Alex used her voice to speak up about the pay gap. Have you ever used your voice to speak up for something you believe in or to help someone else?

What do you think it means to be a leader? What are some qualities that make a good leader? Do you see yourself as a leader in any way?

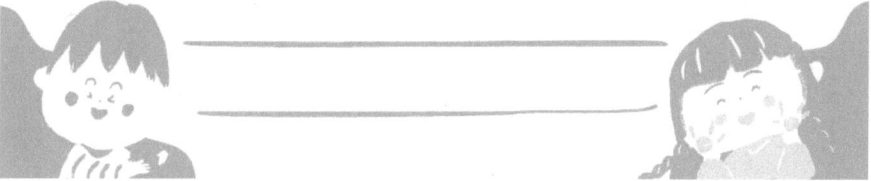

The fight for equal pay was a long and difficult one. What are some challenges you've faced in your life that took time and effort to overcome? How did you stay motivated?

_____

_____

_____

_____

_____

_____

Chapter 12: Alex Morgan Off the Field

> *"The future belongs to those who believe in the beauty of their dreams." - Eleanor Roosevelt*

Hobbies and Interests

When Alex isn't dazzling on the soccer field, she has a whole bunch of other tricks up her sleeve. It turns out this soccer superstar is a multi-talented dynamo who loves to have fun and explore new adventures off the pitch.

One of Alex's favorite pastimes is reading. She loves to curl up with a good book, getting lost in fantastical worlds and meeting exciting characters. Whether it's a thrilling mystery, a heartwarming romance, or an inspirational biography, Alex loves to dive into stories that transport her to new places and teach her new things.

When she's not reading or writing, Alex loves to spend time outdoors. She's a big fan of hiking, exploring trails, and soaking up the sunshine. She's even been known to go camping, sleeping under the stars and roasting marshmallows around a campfire. It's like a real-life adventure, with nature as her playground.

Although it isn't the end of Alex's interests. Additionally, she is a foodie who is constantly looking to expand her culinary horizons. She finds great joy in the kitchen, where she can try out new recipes and create delectable meals for those she loves. The outcome is delicious, but it's more like a science experiment.

And let's not forget her love for animals. Alex has a furry friend named Blue, a sweet and cuddly pup who's always by her side. She loves taking Blue for walks, playing fetch in the park, and snuggling up on the couch for movie nights. It's like having a built-in best friend who's always there for you, no matter what.

Alex is a true renaissance woman, with a wide range of interests and passions. She's not afraid to try new things, to explore her creativity, and to have fun along the way. She's a reminder that life is an adventure, and it's up to us to make the most of it.

Philanthropic Work

Alex Morgan's heart is as big as her soccer skills! She's not just a champion on the field, but also a champion for those in need. She uses her fame and fortune to help others, like a superhero swooping in to save the day.

One of Alex's biggest passions is helping kids. She knows that every child deserves a chance to dream big, to play, to learn, and to grow. So, she supports organizations like the Boys & Girls Clubs of America, which provide safe and fun places for kids to hang out, learn new skills, and make friends.

Alex also works with charities that fight childhood hunger. She knows that no child should go to bed hungry, and she's determined to do her part to make sure every kid has a full belly and a happy heart. She visits food banks, donates money to feeding programs, and even helps pack meals for those in need. It's like a giant pizza party, but instead of just eating pizza, she's helping to make sure everyone gets a slice.

And that's not all of Alex's kindness. She's also a big animal lover. The causes that she believes in include those that help abused and neglected animals, such as animal shelters and wildlife sanctuaries. She went so far as to adopt a wonderful puppy named Blue, who is now considered a member of the family.

Alex believes that everyone can make a difference in the world, no matter how big or small. She encourages kids to find a cause they care about and get involved. Whether it's volunteering at a local shelter, donating to a charity, or simply spreading kindness to others, everyone can do their part to make the world a better place.

Alex is a role model not just for her athletic achievements, but also for her big heart and her willingness to help others. She shows that being a champion isn't just about winning games; it's about making a positive impact on the world. She's an inspiration to us all, proving that even the smallest actions can make a big difference.

Inspiring the Next Generation

Alex Morgan doesn't just want to win championships; she wants to change the world, one soccer ball at a time. She knows that her influence extends far beyond the field, and she uses her platform to inspire the next generation of athletes and dreamers.

For Alex, inspiring young people is like planting seeds of hope and watching them bloom into something beautiful. She wants to show kids that anything is possible if you set your mind to it, work hard, and never give up on your dreams.

One of the ways Alex inspires the next generation is through her actions on the field. When she scores a goal, it's not just about adding another point to the scoreboard; it's about showing kids that they can achieve their dreams if they work hard and persevere. Every time she dives to save a ball or makes a daring pass, she's demonstrating the importance of teamwork, dedication, and never giving up.

Beyond her physical accomplishments, though, Alex has an impact that is immeasurable. Off the pitch, she is an inspiration for the way she fights for justice, fairness, and equality. For young people, she exemplifies the power of standing up for one's values, no matter how challenging or controversial they may be. By doing so, she encourages students to find their unique voices and utilize them to change the world.

Alex is a champion for girls and women in sports. She knows firsthand the challenges they face, from discrimination to unequal pay. She uses her platform to advocate for change, to create a more level playing field where all athletes can thrive. When young girls see Alex fighting for equality, it gives them the courage to fight for their own dreams and aspirations.

But Alex's impact isn't limited to just girls and women. She inspires kids of all genders and backgrounds to dream big, to push their limits, and to never give up on themselves. She shows them that with hard work, dedication, and a positive attitude, they can achieve anything they set their minds to.

Alex is also a strong advocate for education. She knows that knowledge is power, and she encourages kids to stay in school, work hard, and pursue their passions. She believes that education is the key to unlocking opportunities and creating a better future for themselves and their communities.

Alex's commitment to inspiring the next generation goes beyond just words. She actively participates in programs that support young athletes, such as youth soccer clinics, mentorship programs, and scholarships. She visits schools, speaks at conferences, and uses her social media platforms to connect with young people and share her message of hope and inspiration.

She also partners with organizations that promote youth sports and education, like the Boys & Girls Clubs of America and the Women's Sports Foundation. She believes that every child deserves the opportunity to participate in sports, regardless of their background or socioeconomic status.

Alex Morgan's legacy is not just about her achievements on the soccer field; it's about the countless lives she has touched and the countless dreams she has inspired. She's a beacon of hope, a champion of change, and a role model for generations to come. She's proof that with passion, dedication, and a little bit of magic, anything is possible.

Besides soccer, Alex has many hobbies and interests. What are some of your hobbies and interests outside of school or sports?

Alex is involved in philanthropic work, which means she helps others. Have you ever volunteered your time or helped someone in need? How did it make you feel?

Alex uses her platform to inspire the next generation. Who are some people in your community who inspire you? How do they inspire you?

_____

_____

_____

_____

_____

_____

What do you think it means to be a well-rounded person? What are some things you do to explore your interests and learn new things?

_____

_____

_____

_____

_____

_____

Alex is not just an athlete, but also a writer, a businesswoman, and a mom. What are some different roles you play in your life? How do they make you a unique and interesting person?

Chapter 13: What Makes Alex Morgan Special

> *"Dream big, work hard, stay focused, and surround yourself with good people." - Alex Morgan*

Her Determination

What distinguishes Alex Morgan and sets her apart from others? Does her remarkable speed on the soccer pitch, her exceptional goal-scoring skills, or her leadership qualities encourage her teammates? Indeed, it encompasses all of these aspects and more. Alex Morgan possesses exceptional qualities that set her apart, including her unwavering resolve, her exemplary guidance, and her profound devotion to the sport. Now, let's explore the exceptional qualities that make Alex an outstanding role model and athlete.

To begin, let us discuss the unwavering resolve exhibited by Alex Morgan. Since early childhood, Alex possessed a clear aspiration to pursue a career as a professional soccer player. She was not merely satisfied with playing for enjoyment; she aspired to be the most exceptional. Her resolve was apparent in all of her actions. Upon commencing her soccer journey, she diligently engaged in relentless practice. She honed her skills in dribbling, shooting, and passing. She diligently rehearsed during her personal time, apart from the scheduled team practices. While other children may have been engaging in recreational activities such as playing video games or watching television, Alex was actively refining her abilities on the field.

One of the most impressive examples of Alex's determination came when she faced injuries. Injuries are a tough part of being an athlete. They can be painful, frustrating, and sometimes even make you doubt your ability to continue. But not Alex. When she tore her ACL, a serious knee injury, many people thought it might slow her down. But Alex didn't let it stop her. She focused on her recovery with the same determination she showed on the field. She followed her physical therapy plan rigorously, worked on regaining her strength, and made a triumphant return to the game. Her determination to overcome adversity is a true testament to her character.

Another example of Alex's determination is how she balanced soccer with her education. Alex understood that being successful in soccer didn't mean she could neglect her studies. She worked hard in school, managing her time between classes, homework, and soccer practice. This balance was not easy, but Alex's determination to excel in both areas showed that she was willing to put in the effort needed to achieve her goals.

Alex's determination also shines through in her relentless pursuit of excellence. Even after achieving so much success, she never stopped pushing herself to be better. Whether it was working on a specific skill, studying her opponents, or maintaining peak physical condition, Alex always looked for ways to improve. This mindset of continuous improvement is a key part of what makes her special.

Her Leadership

Leadership is about more than simply having top performance; it's about motivating and encouraging others around you. When it comes to leading, Alex is an expert. She motivates her colleagues by working tirelessly and staying focused, never giving up. She is well regarded by both her teammates and coaches for her good attitude and steadfast dedication to the squad.

One of the ways Alex demonstrates her leadership is through her actions during games. When the team is down, and the pressure is on, Alex steps up. She encourages her teammates, reminding them of their strengths and the importance of sticking together. She never blames others for mistakes; instead, she focuses on what they can do better as a team. Her ability to stay calm and composed under pressure helps her teammates feel more confident and motivated.

Alex's leadership extends beyond the soccer field. She is a vocal advocate for gender equality in sports. She uses her platform to speak out about the importance of equal pay and opportunities for female athletes. By doing so, she not only fights for her own rights but also for the rights of future generations of female athletes. Her courage to stand up for what she believes in is a powerful example of leadership.

Another aspect of Alex's leadership is her mentorship. She takes the time to guide and support younger players, both on her team and in the wider soccer community. She shares her experiences, offers advice, and provides encouragement. Her willingness to help others grow and succeed makes her a beloved figure in the soccer world.

Her Passion

An athlete's passion is what keeps them going when the going gets difficult. It's hard to look at Alex and not see her enthusiasm for soccer. She clearly loves the game; it shows in her training and her performance.

Alex's passion for soccer started at a young age. She fell in love with the sport the first time she kicked a ball, and that passion has only grown over the years. Her excitement and enthusiasm are infectious, inspiring those around her to share in her love for the game. Whether she's scoring a game-winning goal or simply practicing drills, Alex's joy and passion are always on display.

This passion extends beyond her own performance. Alex is deeply committed to the growth and development of women's soccer. She works tirelessly to promote the sport, increase its visibility, and create more opportunities for young girls to play. Her efforts have helped raise the profile of women's soccer worldwide, inspiring countless young athletes to pursue their dreams.

One of the most touching examples of Alex's passion is her involvement in the community. She regularly participates in soccer clinics, youth programs, and charity events. She loves sharing her knowledge and enthusiasm with young fans, encouraging them to follow their dreams and stay active. Her genuine care and dedication to giving back make her a true role model.

Alex's passion is also reflected in her resilience. When faced with setbacks, she doesn't lose heart. Instead, she uses those challenges as motivation to work even harder. Her passion for the game keeps her focused and determined, no matter what obstacles she encounters.

Alex has pursued several responsibilities within the soccer community in addition to her athletic successes, driven by her enthusiasm for the sport. Her life's journey and the wisdom she's gained are chronicled in books aimed to young readers. These novels are about more than simply her achievements; they are also about the passion, perseverance, and hard work that it takes to realize one's goals. Athletes of all ages find inspiration and motivation in Alex's words.

As we look at what makes Alex Morgan special, it's clear that her determination, leadership, and passion are key ingredients. These qualities have not only made her a standout soccer player but also a role model and inspiration for many. Her journey shows us that with hard work, a positive attitude, and a love for what you do, you can achieve amazing things.

Alex's story is a reminder that dreams are worth pursuing, no matter how big they may seem. Her determination teaches us the importance of never giving up, even when faced with challenges. Her leadership shows us the value of supporting and uplifting those around us. And her passion reminds us to find joy in what we do and to share that joy with others.

As you follow your own dreams, remember the lessons from Alex Morgan's journey. Stay determined, be a leader, and let your passion guide you. Whether you're playing sports, studying, or pursuing any other goal, these qualities will help you succeed. And just like Alex, you can inspire others along the way.

Alex Morgan's journey is far from over. She continues to set new goals, face new challenges, and inspire those around her. Her story is a testament to the power of determination, leadership, and passion. It shows us that with the right mindset and a lot of hard work, we can achieve anything we set our minds to.

So, dream big, work hard, and never give up. Let Alex Morgan's story be a guide and inspiration as you pursue your own dreams. Remember that you have the power to achieve great things and to make a difference in the world. Just like Alex, you can be a leader, a role model, and a source of inspiration for others. Keep believing in yourself, and always let your passion shine through.

The book describes Alex's determination, leadership, and passion. What are some qualities you admire about yourself?

_____

_____

_____

_____

_____

_____

Alex shows that hard work and dedication can help you achieve your goals. Have you ever worked hard to achieve something you wanted? What was it?

_____

_____

_____

_____

_____

Alex is a leader on and off the field. Have you ever been a leader in a group or activity? What did you do to help your group succeed?

What do you think makes someone a good teammate? How can you be a better teammate to your friends or classmates?

Alex's passion for soccer is contagious. What are you passionate about? How does your passion make you feel?

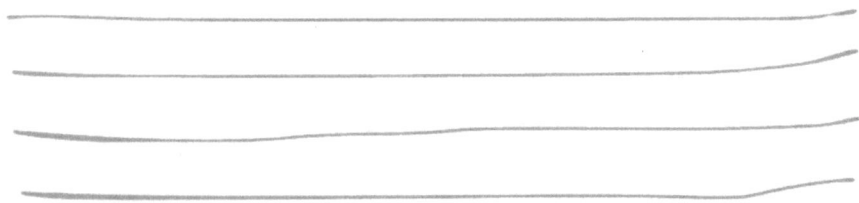

Chapter 14: Alex Morgan's Legacy

> *"Champions are made from something they have deep inside them – a desire, a dream, a vision."* – Mahatma Gandhi

As we reflect on the incredible journey of Alex Morgan, it's clear that her legacy extends far beyond her numerous accomplishments on the soccer field. Alex Morgan is not just a true champion; she is a role model for all and continues to inspire countless people around the world. Let's dive into what makes Alex's legacy so impactful and what might be next for this remarkable athlete.

Alex Morgan is undoubtedly a true champion. Her list of achievements is impressive and speaks volumes about her talent, dedication, and perseverance. From winning World Cups to earning Olympic gold medals, Alex's career is filled with moments of triumph. She has scored countless goals, broken records, and earned the respect of her peers and fans alike. But being a champion is about more than just winning titles; it's about the journey and the character built along the way.

One of the most memorable highlights of Alex's career was the 2015 FIFA Women's World Cup. The U.S. Women's National Team faced tough competition, but Alex's leadership and determination helped propel the team to victory. The moment when they lifted the World Cup trophy was not just a win for the team but a win for all the fans who believed in them. Alex's performance throughout the tournament was stellar, and she emerged as one of the standout players, showcasing her skill, speed, and tenacity.

In 2012, Alex helped the U.S. team secure a gold medal at the London Olympics. Her critical goals and assists were crucial to the team's success. These achievements highlight her ability to perform under pressure and deliver when it matters most. Her drive to succeed and her relentless pursuit of excellence make her a true champion.

Alex Morgan is also a role model for all. Her impact reaches beyond the soccer field, inspiring young athletes and fans around the world. She embodies the values of hard work, determination, and resilience. Her journey from a young girl with big dreams in Diamond Bar, California, to a global soccer superstar shows that anything is possible with dedication and passion.

Alex's influence is particularly significant for young girls who aspire to play sports. She has shown them that they can compete at the highest levels and achieve their dreams. Her advocacy for gender equality and equal pay in sports has also made her a powerful voice for change. Alex has used her platform to speak out on important issues, fighting for fairness and inspiring others to do the same.

Beyond her athletic achievements, Alex's commitment to giving back is another reason she is a role model. She frequently participates in soccer clinics, youth programs, and charity events. She loves connecting with young fans, encouraging them to stay active and pursue their dreams. Her genuine care and dedication to making a positive impact on the community make her a beloved figure.

One of Alex's significant contributions off the field is her work as an author. She has written books for young readers, sharing her experiences and the lessons she's learned. Through her books, Alex aims to inspire and motivate the next generation of athletes. Her stories are filled with messages of perseverance, teamwork, and the importance of following your passion.

As we think about what's next for Alex Morgan, it's exciting to consider the possibilities. Even as she continues to excel on the soccer field, Alex is always looking for new challenges and opportunities. She has expressed interest in pursuing roles that allow her to give back to the sport and continue to inspire others. Whether it's through coaching, mentoring, or expanding her work in advocacy, Alex's future is bright.

Alex has also hinted at exploring opportunities in the media and entertainment industries. Her charisma and passion for storytelling could make her a natural fit for roles in sports broadcasting or even acting. Whatever path she chooses, there's no doubt that Alex will approach it with the same determination and dedication that have defined her soccer career.

Moreover, Alex's commitment to promoting women's sports and fighting for equality will undoubtedly remain a central part of her legacy. She will likely continue to use her voice to advocate for positive change, working to ensure that future generations of female athletes have the opportunities they deserve. Her work in this area is crucial and will have a lasting impact on the world of sports.

As Alex Morgan's journey continues, we can expect her to keep breaking barriers and setting new standards of excellence. Her story is far from over, and she will undoubtedly continue to inspire and motivate others with her actions and achievements. Whether on the soccer field or in other endeavors, Alex's legacy will be one of greatness, leadership, and unwavering commitment to making a difference.

In reflecting on Alex Morgan's legacy, we are reminded of the power of dreams and the importance of hard work and determination. Alex's story shows us that with passion and perseverance, we can achieve our goals and inspire others along the way. She is a true champion, a role model for all, and a shining example of what it means to live with purpose and integrity.

As you pursue your own dreams, remember the lessons from Alex Morgan's journey. Stay determined, be a leader, and let your passion guide you. No matter what challenges you face, believe in yourself and keep pushing forward. Just like Alex, you have the potential to achieve amazing things and make a positive impact on the world.

Therefore, aspire to achieve ambitious goals, exert significant effort, and persist unwaveringly. Allow Alex Morgan's narrative to serve as a wellspring of inspiration and drive as you navigate your own journey. Keep in mind that you possess the ability to establish your own enduring reputation, one that will motivate others and have a lasting impact. It is important to constantly bear in mind, as Alex suggests, the need to have ambitious aspirations, put in diligent effort, maintain concentration, and associate oneself with others of high moral character.

START A JOURNAL WHERE YOU WRITE DOWN
IMPORTANT LIFE LESSONS YOU'VE LEARNED
FROM BOOKS, EXPERIENCES, OR PEOPLE YOU
ADMIRE. REFLECT ON HOW YOU CAN APPLY
THOSE LESSONS TO YOUR OWN LIFE.

Made in United States
Troutdale, OR
02/01/2025

28558994R00106